The English Setter

– A Complete Anthology of the Dog –

1860-1940

ISBN No.
978-14455-2598-3 (Paperback)
978-14455-2718-5 (Hardback)

British Library Cataloguing-in-Publication Data
A catalogue record for this book is available from
the British Library

VDB
www.vintagedogbooks.com

Contents

Containing chapters from the following sources:

THE ENGLISH AND IRISH SETTERS.

These two varieties differ but slightly from each other in shape; but the Irish dog stands a little higher on his legs, and is said to be the hardiest breed of the two. In *colour*, the pure Irish Setter is dark red, of two shades, one being nearly black, and the other a kind of chestnut; he should have little or no white about him. According to Youatt, he may also be lemon-colour, or white patched with deep chestnut, provided he has a black nose and palate; but it is a question whether dogs with these colours have not been crossed either with the Pointer or the English Setter.

The English Setter has evidently much of the Pointer about him, for he has all the colours peculiar to that breed; namely, white as a predominating colour, spotted, and sometimes ticked with lemon-colour, liver, yellow, red, or black, &c.

The coat should be wavy; but neither very curly, like the Water-spaniel, nor so thick as in the Newfoundland. As this dog is chiefly used on rough ground, which is unsuited to the feet of the Pointer, his legs should be well feathered, and his feet clothed with hair, as a protection from heather and thorns.

The "flag," or tail, should be well furnished with hair, which should droop, rather than be thick or bushy.

In form, the Setter resembles the Pointer; but his *head* is smaller, the *jowl* less developed, the *loins* apparently not so strong, and he is altogether a lighter, leggier, and less compactly made dog; notwithstanding which, he is faster, has a freer range, and can stand more work. For this reason he is preferred on the moors, while the Pointer, being usually under better command, is employed for partridge-shooting in enclosed country. The nose of the Setter is also unquestionably inferior to that of the Pointer; but as the scent of the Grouse is strong, compared to that of the Partridge, this defect is counterbalanced by the freer range.

In intelligence, if not in docility, the Setter greatly surpasses the Pointer, and performing-dogs of this breed may sometimes be seen in the streets of London. The Setter also makes an excellent companion, unlike the Pointer, who is a stupid and uninteresting dog when not in the field.

The breaking of the Pointer and Setter is described elsewhere.

THE ENGLISH SETTER.

Since the first publication of the articles on the various breeds of dogs in the *Field*, during the years 1865-6, the strain of English setters known by the name of "Laverack," from the gentleman who bred them, has carried all before it, both on the show bench and in the public field trials which have been annually held. For this high character it is greatly indebted to the celebrated Countess, who was certainly an extraordinary animal, both in appearance and at work; for until she came out the only Laverack which had shone to advantage was Sir R. Garth's Daisy, a good average bitch. Though small, Countess was possessed of extraordinary pace, not perhaps quite equal to that of the still more celebrated pointer Drake, but approaching so closely to it that his superiority would be disputed by many of her admirers. On referring to her portrait accompanying this chapter, it will be seen that her frame, though on short legs, is full of elegance, and her beautiful head and neck are absolutely perfect. With her high pace she combined great power of endurance, and her chief fault was that she never could be fully depended on; for, when fresh enough to display her speed and style to the full, she would break away from her master and defy his whistle until she had taken her fling over a thousand acres or so. On a good scenting day it was a high treat to see her at work; but, like most other fast gallopers, she would sometimes flush her game on a bad scenting day, and then she would be wild with shame. An instance of this occurred at the Bala field trials of 1872, when, on her appearance in the stake for braces with her sister Nellie, both of these bitches were utterly beyond the control of Mr. Buckell, who worked them, Nellie even chasing a bird like a raw puppy. To get rid of this wildness, they were worked hard in the day which intervened between their appearance in the braces and Countess's trial in the Rhiwlas Stakes, when she came out as stale as a poster, and was only placed third to Ranger and Belle. Still, though manifestly beaten, she evidently was so from bad judgment alone on the part of those who managed her; and she only injured the character of the stock to which she belongs so far as to show that, like most high-couraged setters, they require a certain amount of work to keep them steady, which it appears she had not had. Nellie (the sister) was of the same size, but not so fast nor so elegant; still she was good enough to beat the crack on one occasion at Vaynol in 1872, but on most days she would have stood no chance against Countess. She served to show that Countess was not wholly exceptional, as was sometimes alleged by the detractors of the "Laverack"; and these two bitches, together with Sir R. Garth's Daisy, may fairly be adduced as indicating that at all events these Laverack bitches were quite first-class. No, dog, however, of the pure breed has yet put in an appearance at any field trial with any pretension to high form, but several winners have appeared half or quarter bred of that strain. For example, Mr. Statter's Bruce, by Dash (Laverack) out of owner's Rhœbe, and his Rob Roy, by Fred II. (also Laverack) out of the same bitch, may be adduced; but Dick and Dan, by Duke (of the Corbet and Graham strain) out of Rhœbe, were far superior to these dogs, and serve to show that, at all events as crosses for other breeds, the Laveracks are not to be so highly recommended as Mr. Lort and other disciples of the "Laverack" school would lead us to believe. The cross which has been most successful is that with Mr. Lort's, Sir R. Garth's, and Mr. Paul Hackett's blood, culminating in the third remove from the Laverack kennel in Mr. Macdona's Ranger. This dog was fully as fast as Countess, with a keener nose and far better temperament, being, when in form, as steady and dependable as a steam locomotive. Mr. Macdona's favourite may be classed A 1 among the field trial winners in a quintet including Drake, Countess, Dash II., and Belle; the Irish setter,

5

Plunket, approaching them very nearly, but not quite reaching their level. Roll and Frank, who won several prizes on the show bench, are of the same cross as the grandsire of Ranger, all being out of Lort's Dip by a Laverack dog, and these last being all the same blood, as I shall presently show, though their sires are respectively named Rock and Fred II. Roll was a grand dog in shape, with the exception of his loin, in which a certain amount of slackness was displayed when a little out of condition, as he generally was when shown, being a shy feeder. I am told by Mr. Lort, who shot over him for some time, that he was as good in the field as on the bench, but when I tried him he had no nose whatever. His pace was very great, with the usual Laverack quiet trail of flag; and the spaniel-like character peculiar to the Laverack dogs is also quite lost in him by the cross with the Anglesea bitch Dip. Next to this cross comes that with the Corbet and Graham strains as shown in Mr. Brewis's Dash II., who this year (1877) has beaten Ranger in two out of three stakes at Shrewsbury and Horseheath, and whose portrait I have selected, with that of Countess, to illustrate this breed as excellent specimens of the high-bred English setter, though the dog is still, in my opinion, a little too spaniel-like in the shape of the body. He and his sister, Daisy, also a field trial winner, are by Laverack's Blue Prince, out of Armstrong's Old Kate. This bitch is by Laverack's old Blue Dash, out of E. Armstrong's Kate, sister to his Duke, the sire of Dan, about whose stock a great deal has been written in the highest terms by "Percival" and "Setter" in the *Field* and elsewhere, and by Mr. Purcell Llewellyn, who has used him as a stud dog almost exclusively to cross with his Laverack bitches, after purchasing him at a very high price, together with his brother Dick, from Mr. Statter at the Shrewsbury meeting of 1871. The opinions expressed by these gentlemen must be taken *cum grano salis*, as they are manifestly interested in the breed, which they style as *par excellence* "the field trial breed" from the successes obtained by its component parts at these trials. I shall therefore confine myself in my remarks on it to their public performances as observed by myself and others, disregarding all private opinions in this as in all other cases, from my experience of the little reliance to be placed upon them.

The most remarkable feature in the Laverack breed of setters is the extraordinary extent to which in-breeding has been carried, as shown in the pedigree of Countess, given by Mr. Laverack in his book on the setter. By examining this carefully, it will be seen that every animal in it is descended from Ponto and Old Moll, which were obtained by Mr. Laverack in 1825 from the Rev. A. Harrison, who lived near Carlisle, and who had kept the breed pure for thirty-five years. Four names only besides these two are found in the right hand column, and these four are all descended from Ponto and Old Moll, as will be seen at a glance by referring to the names in italic in the middle of the table. Thus it appears that they alone formed Mr. Laverack's breed, though he often stated that he had tried the introduction of alien blood, but finding it not to answer he had abandoned the produce, and resorted again to the original stock. This has led to the belief that the pedigree is incorrect, but he was very positive in his statement. If correct, it certainly is the most remarkable case of breeding in and in I ever met with.

6

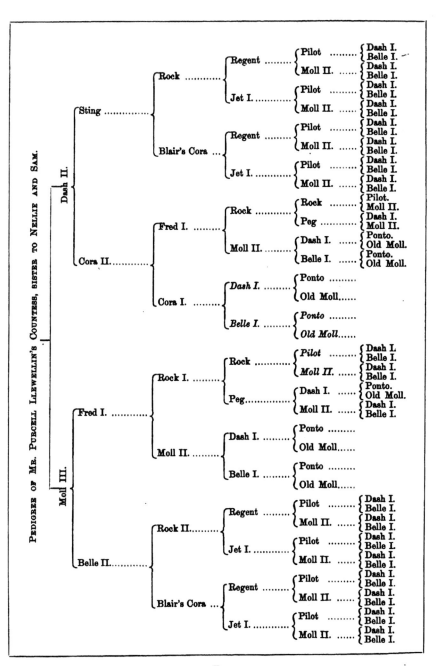

The supporters of the opinion that Mr. Laverack's pedigrees are incorrect adduce two arguments against him, first, that he has, shortly before his death, given different pedigrees of his stud dogs; and, secondly, that the average duration of life in each generation, from Dash and Belle, to Countess, Nellie, and Sam, was fully nine years, which is certainly very remarkable, though within the bounds of possibility. The first of these arguments does not go for much, as we all know that after a man has passed his 70th year his memory is not often to be relied on; and, as to the second, though *per se* highly improbable, it is, as I have above remarked, by no means impossible. But the discussion of this point is of little practical interest, the "Laverack" breed having been sufficiently tested in practice to stand on its own merits without regard to any theoretical opinions. No one disputes that it is in-bred to an extent which few would care to imitate; and if it could be proved that a cross had been occasionally introduced, instead of being considered to have lost in value, I should estimate it more highly. The discussion, therefore, is purely one of curiosity, and need not influence any breeder in his selection of a breeding stud.

To this in-breeding is, no doubt, to be attributed the fact that the Laverack setters are very difficult to rear, and that a large proportion of them die of distemper. Whether or no the average working "form" of the breed is a high one, is very difficult to decide; but, undoubtedly, Countess and her sister Nelly were grand specimens of the high-bred setter. Nearly all the pure Laverack dogs which have been shown are too spaniel-like in shape to please my eye, the only exceptions I remember being Prince and Rock, and to some extent the well-known Sam, brother to Countess and Nellie; nevertheless, they have not the spaniel carriage of the flag alluded to above, which is in them generally trailed like that of the fox, and without any lashing or feathering. Probably it is owing to the excessive in-breeding of the Laveracks injuring their health that they have not succeeded as well as might be expected as sires; but at all events, from whatever cause, a good deal of disappointment has been felt by breeders on that score. Nevertheless, for work the breed still maintains the high character gained for it in its purity by Countess, Nellie, and Garth's Daisy, and for its crosses by Ranger, Dick, Dash II., Field's Daisy, Prince, Ginx's Baby, Glen, Rhoda, Druid, Norah and Nora, and, last, but not least, that excellent little bitch, Mr. Lloyd Price's Queen, by Blue Prince out of the Rev. S. East's Quaver II.—bred by that gentleman from his own old Shropshire blood.

A great many different strains of English setters might be adduced from all parts of the country, but notably from the north of England, with claims superior to those of Mr. Laverack's strain, up to the time of the institution of field trials. Among these were the Graham and Corbet breeds, those of the Earl of Tankerville, Lord Waterpark, Mr. Bishop, Mr. Bayley, Mr. Lort, Mr. Jones (of Oscott), Major Cowan, Mr. Withington, Mr. Paul Hackett, and Mr. Calver, the last two being a good deal crossed with Gordon blood. None of these strains were, however, so generally known beyond the immediate circle of their owners' friends as to have gained a universal reputation; and it was not till the public appearance of Mr. Garth's Daisy, and afterwards that of Mr. Purcell Llewellyn's Countess and Nelly, that the Laverack strain attained its present high reputation. Before Daisy came out, Mr. Garth had produced a brace of very bad ones at Stafford in 1867; and it was with considerable prejudice against them that the above celebrated bitches first exhibited their powers, in spite of the high character given of them by Mr. Lort, Mr. Withington, and other well-known sportsmen who had shot over them for years. It is Mr. Lort's opinion that Mr. Withington possessed better dogs than even Countess; but it must not be forgotten that private trials are generally more flattering than those before the public.

I come now to consider the value of Mr. Llewellyn's "field trial" strain, as they are somewhat grandiloquently termed by their "promoters," or as I shall term them, the "Dan-Laveracks," being all either by Dan out of Laverack bitches, or by a Laverack dog out of a sister to Dan. As a proof of the superiority of this cross to the pure Laveracks "Setter" states, that "during the last two years ten of this breed" (Laveracks), "and ten of the Duke-Rhœbe and Laverack cross have been sent to America; the former including Petrel, winner of the champion prize at Birmingham, Pride of the Border, Fairy, and Victress; the latter including Rock, Leicester, Rob Roy, Dart, and Dora, the same men being owners of both sorts. At the American shows both sorts have appeared, and the Rhœbe blood has always beaten the Laverack. At field trials no Laverack has been entered; but, first, second, and third prizes were gained at their last field trials, in the champion stakes, by dogs of the Rhœbe blood, all descended from Mr. Llewellyn's kennel." I confess that, in my opinion, this does not indicate any superiority in the one over the other, as far as regards field trials, since they were not tested together; and, in reference to the superiority of the Dan-Laveracks on the show bench, it is of little interest to my present inquiry, but I unhesitatingly state, that, as far as my judgment and opportunities for forming it go, "Setter" is quite correct. Dan himself was a very fine upstanding and handsome dog, and his stock might therefore be expected to resemble him, while the Laverack dogs are nearly all heavy and lumbering, and the bitches, though very elegant, too small and delicate for perfection. But, as I have above remarked, the Laveracks have not shown very delicate noses in public, and indeed I have always considered them rather deficient than otherwise in this quality, which is the worst point of the setter as compared with the pointer, and should be regarded, therefore, as the first essential in estimating any of its strains. Now, though I have always regarded Duke himself as on the whole a good dog, especially in pace and range, and have estimated Dan and Duke, the result of his cross with Mr. Statter's Rhœbe, favourably, as compared with the Laverack litters as shown in Bruce and Rob Roy, yet I never considered Dan as a good cross for the Laverack bitches, because his sire always showed a want of nose similar to that of the Laveracks themselves. Duke is said by "Setter," and I believe correctly, to have received a high character from Mr. Barclay Field for his nose as exhibited in private, but he was notoriously deficient in this quality when brought before the public, going with his head low, and feeling the foot rather than the body scent. In proof of this defect it is only necessary to say that he was beaten by Hamlet and Young Kent in this quality at Bala in 1867, when the judge gave him only thirty-one out of a possible forty for "nose;" while at Stafford in the following spring Rex found birds twenty yards behind the place where he had left his point, and thereby gained the cup, Sir V. Corbett, the breeder of Duke, being one of the judges, and loud in admiration of Rex's nose, at the same time finding fault with that of Duke. Indeed, this defect was always made the excuse for E. Armstrong's constant interference with him by hand and voice—whether rightly or wrongly I do not pretend to say, but it evidently marked that clever breaker's want of confidence in his dog's nose. Of Rhœbe herself I do not recollect enough to give an opinion as to this quality in her individually; and among her produce I do not remember any but Bruce and Dan that displayed even an average amount of scenting powers. Rob Roy was notoriously deficient in nose; and Dick, brother to Dan, in his second season, was constantly making false points, and is so described in the report of the Southampton Trials of 1872. For these reasons, although I had always considered the Duke-Rhœbe cross superior to the two Laverack-Rhœbe litters, I never expected Dan to get such a good bitch as Norna in point of nose and correct carriage of head and flag, according to my ideas. If Nora, as alleged by her owner and "Setter," as well as by the *Field* reporter at Horseheath, is superior to her, I can only make my apology to Dan, and admit that he has turned out a better sire than I expected, and than might have been gathered from the performances of Laura, Leda, and Druid, at the Devon and Cornwall, and Sleaford trials of 1874, which I saw. These two bitches were slow and without any style whatever, while the dog, though moderately fast, was well beaten by Ranger at Sleaford at all points.

In 1875 it is true he turned the tables on Mr. Macdona's dog, who was out of all form at that meeting, but he could only get second to Viscount Downe's Sam, who was consequently at once added to Mr. Llewellin's kennel. Taking into consideration that the dogs which have been exhibited by Mr. Llewellin are picked from a very large kennel, and that as far as I have seen them perform, they have not proved themselves to be above the average, I can only come to the conclusion that Dan has not done any great good in improving the Laveracks, except in size and looks. Neither do I place him or any of his stock in the first rank of field trials winners, which in setters would, I think, include only Countess, Ranger, and Dash II., forming with the pointers Drake and Belle, a quintet in class A1, as remarked above. Dan came out in public only once, it is true, though winning three stakes at that meeting; but he met the same competitors in all, and the victory was virtually a single one. After this he put his shoulder out and never appeared in public, but his brother Dick, who was coupled with him in the braces, and went equally well with him in the short trial accorded them, did nothing worth speaking of next year, except to win the brace prize at Southampton, "by a succession of false points, in which he was splendidly backed" by his companion Ruby; and to divide the Stoneham Stakes with his only competitor Robin, "neither being able to find birds," though Dick "made many points, all of which turned out to be at nothing," according to the report in the *Field*, which is no doubt worthy of all credit from the well known ability of the writer. Moreover, Dan at Shrewsbury had a very narrow escape of defeat by Rake, as recorded by myself at the time, so that on mature reflection I have no hesitation in placing him below the first class; but possibly he is entitled to rank in the second along with Plunket and his son and daughter, Kite and Music (Irish), together with Kate, Rex and Lang (Gordons). To them may probably be added the Dan-Laveracks Nora and Norah, and also Die, the last two winners respectively at Shrewsbury and Horseheath of the puppy stakes, all more or less crossed with the late Mr. Laverack's strain. To sum up, therefore, it may be safely alleged that his setters have been of great service to sportsmen in giving pace and style when crossed with other breeds.

The *points* of the English setter may be described as follows:

1. The *skull* (value 10) has a character peculiar to itself, somewhat between that of the pointer and cocker spaniel, not so heavy as the former's, and larger than the latter's. It is without the prominence of the occipital bone so remarkable in the pointer, is also narrower between the ears, and there is a decided brow over the eyes.

2. The *nose* (value 5) should be long and wide, without any fullness under the eyes. There should be in the average dog setter at least four inches from the inner corner of the eye to the end of the nose. Between the point and the root of the nose there should be a slight depression—at all events, there should be no fullness—and the eyebrows should rise sharply from it. The nostrils must be wide apart and large in the openings, and the end should be moist and cool, though many a dog with exceptionally good scenting powers has had a remarkably dry nose, amounting in some cases to roughness like that of shagreen. In all setters the end of the nose should be black, or dark liver-coloured, but in the very best bred whites or lemon and whites pink is often met with, and may in them be pardoned. The jaws should be exactly equal in length, a "snipe nose," or "pig jaw," as the receding lower one is called, being greatly against its possessor.

3. *Ears, lips*, and *eyes* (value 4). With regard to ears, they should be shorter than the pointer's and rounded, but not so much so as those of the spaniel. The "leather" should be thin and soft, carried closely to the cheeks, so as not to show the inside, without the slightest tendency to prick the ear, which should be clothed with silky hair little more than two inches in length. The lips also are not so full and pendulous as those of the pointer, but at their angles there should be a slight fullness, not reaching quite to the extent of hanging. The eyes must be full of animation, and of medium size, the best colour being a rich brown, and they should be set with their angles straight across.

4. The *neck* (value 6) has not the full rounded muscularity of the pointer, being considerably thinner, but still slightly arched, and set into the head without that prominence of the occipital bone which is so remarkable in that dog. It must not be "throaty," though the skin is loose.

5. The *shoulders* and *chest* (value 15) should display great liberty in all directions, with sloping deep shoulder blades, and elbows well let down. The chest should be deep rather than wide, though Mr. Laverack insists on the contrary formation, italicising the word *wide* in his remarks at page 22 of his book. Possibly it may be owing to this formation that his dogs have not succeeded at any field trial, as above remarked; for the bitches of his breed, notably Countess and Daisy, which I have seen, were as narrow as any setter breeder could desire. I am quite satisfied that on this point Mr. Laverack is altogether wrong. I fully agree with him, however, that the "ribs should be well sprung behind the shoulder," and great depth of the back ribs should be especially demanded.

6. *Back, quarters,* and *stifles* (value 15). An arched loin is desirable, but not to the extent of being "roached" or "wheel-backed," a defect which generally tends to a slow up-and-down gallop. Stifles well bent, and set wide apart, to allow the hind legs to be brought forward with liberty in the gallop.

7. *Legs, elbows,* and *hocks* (value 12). The elbows and toes, which generally go together, should be set straight; and if not, the "pigeon-toe" or inturned leg is less objectionable than the out-turn, in which the elbow is confined by its close attachment to the ribs. The arm should be muscular and the bone fully developed, with strong and broad knees, short pasterns, of which the size in point of bone should be as great as possible (a very important point), and their slope not exceeding a very slight deviation from the straight line. Many good judges insist upon a perfectly upright pastern, like that of the foxhound; but it must not be forgotten that the setter has to stop himself suddenly when at full stretch he catches scent, and to do this with an upright and rigid pastern causes a considerable strain on the ligaments, soon ending in "knuckling over;" hence a very slight bend is to be preferred. The hind legs should be muscular, with plenty of bone, clean strong hocks, and hairy feet.

The *feet* (value 8) should be carefully examined, as upon their capability of standing wear and tear depends the utility of the dog. A great difference of opinion exists as to the comparative merits of the cat and hare foot for standing work. Foxhound masters invariably select that of the cat, and, as they have better opportunities than any other class of instituting the necessary comparison, their selection may be accepted as final. But, as setters are specially required to stand wet and heather, it is imperatively necessary that there should be a good growth of hair between the toes, and on this account a hare foot, well clothed with hair, as it generally is, must be preferred to a cat foot naked, as is often the case, except on the upper surface.

9. The *flag* (value 5) is in appearance very characteristic of the breed, although it sometimes happens that one or two puppies in a well-bred litter exhibit a curl or other malformation, usually considered to be indicative of a stain. It is often compared to a scimitar, but it resembles it only in respect of its narrowness, the amount of curl in the blade of this Turkish weapon being far too great to make it the model of the setter's flag. Again, it has been compared to a comb; but as combs are usually straight, here again the simile fails, as the setter's flag

12

should have a gentle sweep; and the nearest resemblance to any familiar form is to the scythe with its curve reversed. The feather must be composed of straight silky hairs, and beyond the root the less short hair on the flag the better, especially towards the point, of which the bone should be fine, and the feather tapering with it.

10. *Symmetry and quality* (value 5). In *character* the setter should display a great amount of "quality," a term which is difficult of explanation, though fully appreciated by all experienced sportsmen. It means a combination of symmetry, as understood by the artist, with the peculiar attributes of the breed under examination, as interpreted by the sportsman. Thus, a setter possessed of such a frame and outline as to charm an artist would be considered by the sportsman defective in "quality" if he possessed a curly or harsh coat, or if he had a heavy head with pendant bloodhoundlike jowl and throaty neck. The *general outline* is very elegant, and more taking to the eye of the artist than that of the pointer.

11. The *texture and feather* of coat (value 5) are much regarded among setter breeders, a soft silky hair without curl being considered a *sine quâ non*. The feather should be considerable, and should fringe the hind as well as the fore legs.

12. The *colour of coat* (value 5) is not much insisted on among English setters, a great variety being admitted. These are now generally classed as follows, in the order given: (1) Black and white ticked, with large splashes, and more or less marked with black, known as "blue Belton;" (2) orange and white freckled known as orange Belton; (3) plain orange, or lemon and white; (4) liver and white; (5) black and white, with slight tan markings; (6) black and white; (7) liver and white; (8) pure white; (9) black; (10) liver; (11) red or yellow.

ENGLISH SETTERS.

14

THE ENGLISH SETTER.

WHATEVER the origin of the Setter may have been, there can be no possibility of a doubt but that he holds a position second to none in the canine world in the present day. The beauty of the dog's coat and the brilliancy of his colours, coupled with his use and intelligence in the field, cannot fail to make the Setter a favourite with all who really admire and love a good dog. Another important feature in connection with his popularity, and which has been no small support to it, is the amount of national jealousy and prejudice which has been from time to time imported into discussions on the breed, as, naturally enough, each variety finds keen supporters amongst its fellow-countrymen. To explain our meaning we must at once allude to the fact that in the present day Setters are divided into three distinct varieties—viz., the English Setter, the Irish Setter, and the Gordon Setter. This latter breed is recognised as the Scottish national Setter, its origin being traced to Gordon Castle, Aberdeenshire, and will, with its Irish relative, be fully alluded to presently. There was an old Welsh breed, too, of black-and-white Setters which is almost extinct, though frequently pathetically alluded to by veteran sportsman hailing from the Principality in question.

In various localities throughout the country families or strains of Setters from special lines adopted in breeding—doubtless with the object of producing the dog best suited to the country over which they were to be worked—assumed peculiarities distinguishing them from each other, and became known by special names, such as the kennels which became known for breeding good ones. The Earl of Carlisle has a strain, specimens of which have occasionally been shown, and which display strongly-marked Spaniel characteristics, and from the tendency to curl in the coat, the top-knot more or less developed, and their general shape, suggest their having been grafted on the Water Spaniel. In the Marquis of Bute's kennels in the west of Scotland there was long, and probably still is, a strain of black Setters, and numerous kennels of extent had strains specially their own with some distinguishing feature. The Beltons, famous in the northern counties, are a superb race, and form the great base of the now famous Laverack Setter, on which again is founded the majority of the great kennels so favourably known throughout the country, and which has an immense popularity with American sportsmen.

Whether any of the modern and present-day breeders have resorted to a Spaniel cross direct, we are not in a position to state, but that such might be done with advantage in some instances we do not doubt.

In spite, however, of the numerous families into which the Setter is now divided, there can be no doubt that the origin of each was the Spaniel, and it is a curious subject for contemplation that Spain (as will be seen in the chapter on Pointers) should have the credit of supplying us with the three breeds of sporting dogs—Spaniels, Setters, and Pointers —upon which we English so greatly pride ourselves. The credit of improving these dogs

15

is of course our own, but it is impossible to claim any one of them as indigenous to this country, closely identified with it as they are at the time of writing.

Dr. John Caius alludes to the Setter in his work on "English Dogges" under the title of Index, and his classification of it with the Spaniel is a convincing proof of its identity with that animal at the period in which Dr. Caius wrote as follows :—

"Another sort of Dogges be there, serviceable for fowling, making no noise either with foote or with tounge, whiles they followe the game. These attend diligently vpon theyr Master and frame their conditions to such beckes, motions, and gestures, as it shall please him to exhibite and make, either going forward, drawing backeward, inclining to the right hand, or yealding toward the left, (In making mencion of fowles my meaning is of the Partridge and the Quaile) when he hath founde the byrde, he keepeth sure and fast silence, he stayeth his steppes and wil proceede no further, and with a close, couert, watching eye, layeth his belly to the grounde and so creepeth forward like a worme. When he approcheth neere to the place where the birde is, he layes him downe, and with a marcke of his pawes, betrayeth the place of the byrdes last abode, whereby it is supposed that this kinde of dogge is called *Index*, Setter, being in deede a name most consonant and agreeable to his quality. The place being knowne by the meanes of the dogge, the fowler immediatly openeth and spreedeth his net, intending to take them, which being done the dogge at the accustomed becke or vsuall signe of his Master ryseth vp by and by, and draweth neerer to the fowle that by his presence they might be the authors of their owne insnaring, and be ready intangled in the prepared net."

The above extract, though not throwing much light upon the appearance of the breed in the reign of Queen Elizabeth, nevertheless is a proof of its existence; but the following remarks taken from Gervase Markham's "Hunger's Prevention, or the Art of Fowling," which was published in London in 1655, gives a considerable amount of information upon the dog's character and the uses to which it was then placed. Under the heading of "What a Setting Dog is" Gervase Markham writes :—

"Before I wade further into this discourse I show you what a setting dogge is. You shall then understand that a setting dogge is a certaine lusty land spaniell taught by nature to hunt the partridges before, and more then any other chase whatsoever, and that with all eagernesse and fiercenesse, running the fields over and over so lustily and busily as if there were no limit in his desire and furie; yet so qualified and tempered with art and obedience, that when he is in the greatest and eagerest pursute, and seemes to be most wilde and frantike, that yet even then, one hem or sound of his master's voyce makes him presently stand, gaze about him, and looke in his master's face, taking all his directions from it whether to proceede, stand still, or retire. Nay, when he is come even to the very place where his prey is and hath as it were his nose over it, so that it seemes hee may take it up at his owne pleasure, yet is his temperance and obedience so made and framed by arte that presently even on a sudden he either stands still or falles downe flatte upon his belly, without daring once to open his mouth, or make any noyse or motion at all, till that his master come unto him and then proceedes in all things according to his directions and commandements."

This quotation might almost have been taken from a modern work on Setters, as it refers to a class of dog whose duties in the field appear to have little altered during the progress of time. There still seems to have been a considerable looseness in the classification of this breed of dog, and the barrier between the Setter and the Spaniel appears to have been unremoved at a much later time, and the name Setter only applied to dogs broken to set game, and not to those distinguishable by any structural difference in shape or build. In 1697 Nicholas Cox writes of the Setter in "The Gentleman's Recreation" in the following words :—

"The dog which you elect for setting must have a perfect and good scent, and be naturally addicted to the hunting of feathers ; and this dog may be either land spaniel, water spaniel, or mungrel of them both ; either the shallow-flewed hound, tumbler, lurcher, or small bastard mastiff. But there is none better than the land spaniel, being of a good and nimble size, rather small than gross, and of a courageous metal ; which tho' you cannot discern, being young yet, you may may very well know from a right breed, which have been known to be strong, lusty and nimble rangers, of active feet, wanton tails, and busie nostrils, whose tail was without weariness, their search without changeablenesse, and whom no delight did transport beyond fear or obedience."

With reference to the behaviour of this dog in the field, Nicholas Cox remarks as follows in his notes on training the setting dog :—

"You must teach him to come creeping to you with his belly and head close upon the ground, as far or as little away as you think fit. . . . . And this observe in his creeping to you, if he offer to raise his body or head you must not only thrust the rising part down, but threaten him with your angry voice, which if he seem to slight, then add a sharp jerk or two with a whipcord lash. . . . . If you walk abroad with him, and he take a fancy to range, even when he is most busie speak to him, and in the height of his pastime make him fall upon his belly and lie close, and after that make him come creeping to you."

Thus Nicholas Cox succeeds in clearly proving that late in the seventeenth century the Spaniel, or even a mongrel partaking of any breed, was used as a setting dog by British sportsmen. Things do not appear to have undergone any great alteration in the beginning of the next century, for in 1718 one Giles Jacobs produced a book called the "Compleat Sportsman" in which a good deal is said about the setting dog, and sporting in general. The "Compleat Sportsman," which was published in the Savoy, London, was dedicated to Sir Charles Keymis, of Keven-Mabley in the County of Glamorgan, Bart., and may be taken as having been a valuable handbook relating to the laws on sport and dogs at the time when it was written. Mr. Giles Jacobs, however, copies unblushingly from Nicholas Cox, without giving the latter any credit for what he has taken from his works, and the result is that the description of the setting dog which we have quoted above is reproduced in the "Compleat Sportsman." It is, therefore, only reasonable to infer that no change, or, at all events, any material change, had come over the dog during the interval which had expired since Nicholas Cox wrote, or it would have probably been alluded to by Giles Jacobs in his work.

It may here be mentioned in justice to the individual to whom the credit is due, that Robert Dudley, Duke of Northumberland, is supposed to have been the first person to train setting dogs in the manner which has since his time been universally adopted by his successors. His Grace lived about the year 1550, rather earlier than the date at which Dr. Caius wrote, but beyond casual references to him by subsequent writers, nothing is positively known of the system upon which he acted, though from the remarks made it is probable that his ideas were closely carried out by the Setter breakers who came after him.

The "Sportsman's Cabinet," in 1803, devotes a good deal of its space to the subject of Setters, which had evidently by that time taken their rank as a distinct breed of sporting dog. Whether, however, the author is quite correct or not in his assertion that "The dog passing under this denomination [Setter] is a species of Pointer originally produced by a commixture between the Spanish Pointer and the larger breed of English Spaniel," will always be a matter of discussion between persons interested in the breed, as many are to be found who deny the existence of the Pointer cross. This subject may, however, be abandoned for the present, as our desire is now to trace the existence of the English Setter from its first appearance down to modern periods, and at the same time draw what deductions we can from contemporary writers concerning its appearance and value as a sporting dog. Mr. W. Taplin, in the "Sportsman's Cabinet," proceeds to remark subsequently to the preceding quotation, that, " The sporting department of the Setter in the field precisely corresponds with the pursuits and propensities of the Pointer, but with this single variation, that admitting their olfactory sensations to be equally exquisite, and that one can discover and as expeditiously receive and enjoy the particles of scent (or, in other words, the effluvia of the game) as readily and at equal distance with the other, the difference of the sports in which they are individually employed renders it necessary that one should effect upon his legs what the other does by prostration upon the ground, in the very position from which the present appellation of the 'setting dog' is derived. And these are neither more nor less than the pure effect of sporting education ; for as in shoooting with the Pointer the game is constantly expected to rise, so in the use of a setting dog and net the game is required to lie. . . . .

"Although the setting dog is in general used merely for the purpose of taking partridges with the draw-net, yet they are sometimes brought into occasional use with the gun, and are equally applicable to that appropriation, except in turnips, French wheat, standing clover, ling, furze, or other covert, where their sudden drop and point may not be so readily observed."

Personally we attach very great importance to the above extract, for two reasons: first, it is distinctly stated that up to that time Pointers· were the fashionable, or rather the favourite, breed with sportsmen who amused themselves by shooting three-quarters of a century back ; and, secondly, it gives us a good reason for the change which has come over the Setter's behaviour in the field of later years. It is, of course, perfectly well known that the modern Setter usually points his game standing up, as a Pointer does, and the abandonment of netting is unquestionably responsible for this alteration in the method of a Setter carrying out his work. Before, when the sportsman was anxious to net as many birds as he could, it was most essential that they should be as undisturbed as possible, and the presence of a dog would, of course, increase the chances of their being frightened away before the net was fixed for their capture. The chances of the dog being seen by the game were naturally lessened when he lay down, and this, no doubt, was the reason for his being broken to do so. Now things are much altered, and the sportsman only wants the whereabouts of the game to be indicated, so that he may walk them up. There

18

is, however, a perfectly palpable tendency to crouch still observable in many of the best and highest bred Setters of the present day, which is unquestionably accounted for by the former habits of the breed, and the uses to which it was put.

From the following remarks of Mr. Taplin it will be seen that in the early years of this century the Setter was credited (as he is by many in the present day) with being naturally of a timid and nervous temperament, for he writes :—

" It has already been observed that the Setter is in possession of a constitutional timidity which induces him to dread the severity of correction, and, of course, to avoid the means of disgrace; fraught with this irritability their treatment in the field becomes matter of judicious discrimination. Dogs of this description, perpetually alive to the fear of giving offence and incurring bodily punishment, lay claim to every little tender attention as well at home as in the field. Warm, hasty, impetuous sportsmen contribute not unfrequently to their own mortification and disappointment, for many dogs of this disposition corrected in passion or beat with severity are so completely overwhelmed with distress or humiliated with fear that they almost insensibly sink at the feet, and can be prevailed on to hunt no more, or, what is sometimes the case, slink away home without the least chance whatever of being again induced to render further assistance in the sport of the day."

It is an undoubted fact that in the present day many Setters that would otherwise have been invaluable in the field are ruined in their breaking and subsequent education by the severe treatment they receive at the hands of those in whose power they are placed. We are decidedly of the opinion that were less stringent punishment inflicted for trifling offences upon the members of more than one well-known kennel, an even increased reputation would quickly be added to that which it already possesses.

Three years later than the date in which the " Sportsman's Cabinet " was published—viz., in 1806—there was a sale of Setters, the record of which has been handed down to the present day. The prices realised were for the period decidedly good, and as the kennel was the property of a rather famous individual in his way—Daniel Lambert, the historical fat man, who shortly before his death scaled fifty-two stone eleven pounds—and the list, moreover, is valuable as an index to the prices of sporting dogs seventy years ago, we reproduce it at length :—

Peg, a black Setter Bitch ...	....	...	...	...	41	guineas
Punch, a Setter Dog	...	...	...	...	...	26	,,
Brush ,,	...	...	...	...	...	17	,,
Bob ,,	...	...	...	...	...	20	,,
Bell ,,	...	...	...	...	...	32	,,
Bounce ,,	...	...	...	...	...	22	,,
Sam ,,	...	...	...	...	...	26	,,
Charlotte, a Pointer Bitch ...	...	...	...	...	22	,,
Lucy ,,	...	...	...	...	...	12	,,
Total	...	...	...	...	218	,,

This gives an average which would make dog-breeding a successful commercial enterprise even in the present day ; but it is a noticeable fact that the Setters fetched better prices than the Pointers, which must be taken as a proof that the breed was coming up into a higher position in public estimation, or possibly Mr. Lambert's kennel was stronger in Setters than in Pointers.

The date of introduction of the setting dog or Spaniel into this country is not clear. There is no special reference to him in the old forest laws of Canute, which guarded against the keeping of Greyhounds except under stringent conditions of maiming the animals or keeping them at a distance of ten miles from a royal forest, and even Mastiffs kept by farmers and others for the protection of their dwellings had to lose three claws, which was called "expeditating." Spaniels are, however, specially mentioned in a statute anterior to the time of Caius, and the dogs then regarded by the law were Mastiffs, Hounds, Spaniels, and Tumblers. And in a statute of James I. it is provided that no person shall be deemed qualified to keep setting dogs who is not possessed of an inheritance of the value of £10 per annum, a lease for life of £30 per annum, or who is worth £200 per annum, unless he be the son of a baron or knight or heir-apparent to an esquire.

The changed character of the sport of fowling when netting gradually gave way before the increasing use of guns, until it became finally entirely superseded, did no doubt act powerfully in modifying the Setter, and the plastic nature of the dog has been ever since taken advantage of to alter and improve him to suit the constant changes in the conditions of sport. As a factor in the conversion of the ancient Spaniel into the modern Setter, Blaine throws out the suggestion that a cross with one of the *celeres* or swift-footed dogs was resorted to, and that the Pointer is probably a cross between the Spaniel and one or other of the *pugnaces*. To produce the Setter by such a cross, we had in this country the Greyhound and the swift light hound, at one time peculiar to Yorkshire, Cumberland, Northumberland, and probably other northern counties. There were other varieties of the *celeres*, no doubt, but the two mentioned would in our view be the most likely to approve themselves to practical sportsmen. In the absence of proof of such a cross having been resorted to with a special purpose, we content ourselves with pointing out the great reasonableness of Blaine's theory. Granted that the cross was adopted, it is not to be supposed that it was adhered to, but the produce would be bred to the parent strain, the characteristics of which it was purposed should preponderate, and that would be, in this instance, the Spaniel.

It may be argued that the cross with the light hound equally with that by the Greyhound would quite alter the style of hunting, destroy the natural tendency to index or set the game, and the latter cross, to a great extent, destroy the olfactory powers. We do not think such a result would follow, for even if in the first cross such were apparently developed, they would be unequally so in the several members of the litter ; and good judgment in selecting the bitches kept for brood purposes, and wise mating with Spaniel dogs excelling in the qualities partially lost by the cross, would soon restore these in all their former fulness of development, whilst the desired modification of form and other characteristics was sufficiently preserved.

If the theory of the cross with either of those mentioned, or some other of the *celeres* available (but none of which, we are of opinion, would be so suitable to the object in view) be rejected, then we are thrown back on the theory of selection of individuals of the same variety ; for all must admit that, changed as the modern Setter is from all portraits of him in pen, pencil, or by brush, as he existed even so late as the last century, he still in all essentials shows a strong alliance with the Spaniel family. It is not impossible in the production of the modern Setter that he arose from the roughest of Spaniels described by our earliest writers by means of selection alone. None of our domestic animals are so easily changed, and, as it were, moulded to the breeder's will, as the dog, and, in the case under consideration, the time has been more than ample to effect the change.

It is very improbable that we have a better Setter judge than Mr. William Lort, of Fron Goch Hall, Montgomeryshire, and his experience of the breed is practically unlimited. We are, therefore, glad to be able to lay before our readers Mr. Lort's views upon the pro-

DOGS AND PARTRIDGES. (*After Desportes.*)

bability, and also of the desirability, of the Pointer cross, which so many believe to be largely present in most strains of Setters. Mr. Lort writes thus:—

"As to the origin of the Setter, I am not so sure of the correctness of my old and valued friend, Mr. H. Herbert, when he says: 'There is no doubt whatever that the true Setter is a pure strain of unmixed Spaniel blood, the only improvement produced in the breed arising from its judicious cultivation,' &c., &c. I am quite sure that years ago, say from forty to fifty, it was no uncommon thing to get a dip of Pointer blood into the best kennels of Setters. Sometimes it answered well, and though for a generation or two it diminished the coat, not always though at the cost of appearance, it fined and strengthened the stern, giving life and motion to it, and what, whether rightly or wrongly, in early times was thought a good deal of—it rounded the foot.

"I know how shocked some of our modern breeders will be at the idea of their favourites having in their veins a drop of Pointer blood. It is well perhaps that it is not generally known how many fashionable strains have been vitiated with much more objectionable blood than that of the Pointer. I have seen Droppers [cross between a Pointer and Setter], yes, *and dogs bred from Droppers*, possessing exquisite powers of scent, lovely tempers, and great pace. I think there is reason to believe the Spaniel to be the foundation of our present Setter.

"As a case showing that it is possible for cross-bred dogs to breed true, I knew of a black Setter bitch three crosses from Pointer, belonging to Robert Warner, of Leicester Abbey. She was good herself, having all the qualities of a pure Setter, and, curious enough, she bred *well* from either a Setter or Pointer. Mr. Warner gave his keeper (who afterwards came into my service) a brace of black puppies, by a Pointer, of this bitch. They looked all over Pointers, they worked like Pointers, they were excellent Pointers, and were sold, when broken, at 40 gs.—a good price in those days. I myself had Setters from her, and they were good Setters, and showed all Setter characteristics."

A strong confirmation of Mr. Lort's theory is to be found in the subjoined engraving from a painting by the famous French artist, Alexander François Desportes. This great animal painter—born in 1661, and died in 1743—was elected a member of the French Royal Academy of Painting in 1699, and of its Council in 1704. For many years he occupied the Court position of historiographer of the chase, created expressly for him by Louis XIV.; and his pictures, which are very numerous, can hardly be surpassed for their fidelity to Nature. The engraving we reproduce from his pencil is entitled "Dogs and Partridges," and is valuable as distinctly showing that the Pointer had been crossed with the Spaniel before and during his time, and that the result was a dog very like our modern Setter.

It has been before shown that up to the end of the last century Pointers were the more favoured breed of dog by sportsmen, but of late years the Setter has made great progress in public popularity. This may be, to a certain extent, accounted for by the existence of the three varieties—English, Scotch, and Irish—to which allusion has been already made ; but we feel inclined to believe that the natural toughness of this dog's constitution has more to do with the change that has taken place. The thickly-padded feet of the Setter unquestionably render him a preferable dog for all sorts of rough shooting, and on the moors he is far better able to withstand the broken ground and the hard work that has to be encountered than the Pointer, who is more easily fatigued. On the other hand, exception has been taken to the Setter that, though physically stronger than the Pointer, he is not able to work so long without water, and it may be mentioned that this theory was in existence at the time Taplin wrote, for he remarks, with reference to this, his favourite breed :—

"There is an erroneous opinion in circulation that it is a disadvantage to Setters, they cannot continue to hunt long without water; though it is perfectly well known to the most experienced sportsmen they can endure heat, thirst, and fatigue as well, if not better than Pointers ; they are certainly more difficult to break, and when broke are most apt to run wild and unsteady if not frequently hunted."

PUBLIC FIELD TRIALS.

Nearly twenty years later John Scott writes in the "Sportsman's Repository":—

"Many sportsmen prefer the Setter to the Pointer for pheasant shooting, as more active and hardy, having so much of the quality of the Spaniel, and thence not flinching at the thickest coverts. On the moors, and for grouse shooting also, the preference of the Setter is decisive, for although he is said to require much water, and to be unable to endure heat and thirst like the Pointer, the former, from his constitutional activity and the hardness of his feet, is superior in a long day over a rough and uneven surface. From accident, or from that never-failing desire of shining by the intermixture of breeds, with little consideration of the end, Pointers have been crossed with Setters, and Setters with Pointers, but we have not seen any beneficial result. On the score of utility, the Setter can derive no improvement from such a cross; and granting—which, however, is not proved—that the Pointer gains something in regard of usefulness, such advantage will be countervailed by an abatement of size, figure, and stateliness, on which account only, perhaps, he superseded the Setter in the affections of the sportsman. . . . .

"It has been disputed very uselessly whether the Setter or the Pointer have the most powerful nose; but let a sportsman take a thorough good dog of either kind into the field, and he will no longer trouble himself with that dispute. Beyond a doubt, the Setter is the most useful gun dog of the two, but the Pointer is the largest, most stately and showy, and is admired for his rate, his high ranging, and steadiness. The Setter on his part may put in his claim, and more especially when of the pure breed, to his full share of the intelligence, sagacity, and affection for man, which shines so eminently and so delightfully in the Spaniel."

Such remarks as above would seem to betoken a very rapid advance on the part of the Setter in the estimation of sportsmen who used the gun, for it must be borne in mind that not twenty years before it would seem that this dog was only being gradually introduced into this branch of sport, having been more generally used in netting operations up to the commencement of this century. At the period of writing (1880) the Setter is certainly the more successful dog in the field, as his many triumphs in field trial competitions must amply prove. With reference to these trials it may be briefly mentioned that they were instituted by the Kennel Club, which is a Society originated about the year 1869 for the purpose of promoting the general improvement of dogs, dog shows, and dog trials. These latter are unquestionably decided proofs of a dog's capacity for work, and may be regarded as most successful institutions, having been largely patronised by the higher class of sportsmen, who have shown great interest in the trials, and who have in addition entered their dogs largely for competition. The rules for the guidance of field trials are very clearly laid down by the Kennel Club, and being likely to be appreciated by sportsmen who may be desirous of instituting such competitions in their own neighbourhood, a copy of them will be found below.

1. *Management of a Meeting.*—The management of a meeting shall be entrusted to a committee in conjunction with Field Stewards, the latter of whom shall be appointed by the committee before the time of running. The stewards shall decide any disputed question by a majority of those present, subject to an appeal to the committee. No steward shall vote during a meeting in any case relating to his own dogs.

2. *Election of Judges.*—The judge, or judges, shall be elected by the committee, and their names shall be announced as soon as possible after their election. When a judge, from ill-health or any other unexpected cause, is prevented attending a meeting or finishing it, the committee shall have the power of deciding what is to be done.

23

3. *Description of Entry.*—Every subscriber to a stake must name his dog at or before the draw, giving the names of the sire and dam of the dog entered, and also, in puppy stakes, the name of the dam's owner. The secretary shall publish on the card the names of those who are subscribers, but do not comply with these conditions. These nominations shall not be drawn, but must be paid for.

4. *Disqualification.*—For Puppy Stakes, the names, pedigrees, ages, colours, and distinguishing marks of the puppies shall be detailed in writing to the secretary of a meeting at the time of entry. Any puppy whose age, markings, and pedigree shall be proved not to correspond with the entry given shall be disqualified, and the whole of its stakes or winnings forfeited.

5. *Definition of Puppy.*—No dog is to be considered a puppy that was whelped before the 1st of January of the year preceding that of its competing.

6. *Payment of Stakes.*—All money due for nominations taken must be paid on or before the draw, whether the stake fill or not, and although from insufficient description or any other cause, the dogs named may be disqualified. No entry shall be valid unless the amount due for it has been paid in full. For all produce and other stakes where a forfeit is payable no declaration is necessary; the nonpayment of the remainder of the entry money at the time fixed for that purpose is to be considered a declaration of forfeit. The secretary is responsible for the entry money of all dogs whose names appear upon the card.

7. *Alteration of Name.*—If any subscriber should enter a dog by a different name from that in which it shall have last been known in public he shall give notice of the alteration to the secretary at the time of entry, and the secretary shall place on the card both the late and present name of the dog. If notice of the alteration be not given the dog shall be disqualified.

8. *Prefix of "NS."*—Any subscriber taking an entry in a stake, and not prefixing the word "names" to a dog which is not his own property, shall forfeit that dog's chance of the stake. He shall likewise, if requested, deliver in writing to the secretary of the meeting the name of the *bonâ fide* owner of the dog named by him, and this communication is to be produced should any dispute arise in the matter.

9. *Death of Subscribers.*—The death of a subscriber shall only affect his nomination if it occur before the draw, in which case, subject to the exceptions stated below, it shall be void, whether the entries have been made or not, and any money received for forfeits or stakes shall be returned. If he has parted with all interest in the nominations, and dogs not his property are entered, paid for, and drawn in ignorance of his being no longer alive, such entries shall not subsequently be disturbed. When dogs who have been entered in produce stakes change owners with their engagements and with their forfeits paid, the new owner, if otherwise entitled to run them in these stakes, shall not be prevented from doing so by reason of the death of the former owner.

10. *Power to Refuse Entries.*—The committee or stewards of any meeting may reserve to themselves the right of refusing any entries they may think fit to exclude; and no person who has been proved to the satisfaction of the Committee of the Kennel Club to have misconducted himself in any way in connection with dogs, dog shows, or dog trials, will be allowed to compete in any trials that may be held under the Kennel Club Rules.

11. *The Draw.*—Immediately before the dogs are drawn at any meeting, and before nine o'clock on every subsequent evening during the continuance of such meeting, the time and place of putting down the first brace of dogs on the following morning shall be declared. A card or counter bearing a corresponding number shall be assigned to each entry. These numbered cards or counters shall then be placed together and drawn indiscriminately. This classification, once made, shall not be disturbed throughout the meeting, except for the purpose of guarding, or on account of byes. Dogs whose position on the card has been altered in consequence of guarding or of byes must return to their original position in the next round if guarding does not prevent it.

12.—The stakes shall be run in the order they are given in the programme, unless the whole of the competitors or their representatives in the various stakes may agree otherwise—in which case the order may be changed, with the consent of the Stewards or Committee.

13. *Guarding.*—When more than one nomination in a stake is taken in one name, the dogs, if *bonâ fide* the property of the same owner, shall be guarded throughout : this is always to be arranged, as far as possible, by bringing up dogs from below to meet those which are to be guarded. This guarding is not, however, to deprive any dog of a natural bye to which he may be entitled, either in the draw or in running through the stake.

14. *Byes.*—A natural bye shall be given to the lowest available dog in each round. No dog shall run a second such bye in any stake, unless it is unavoidable. When a dog is entitled to a bye, either natural or accidental, his owner or nominator may run any dog he pleases with him.

24

15. *Postponement of Meeting.*—A meeting appointed to take place on a certain day, may, if a majority of the Committee and Stewards (if appointed) consider the weather unfit, be postponed from day to day ; but if the running does not commence within the current week all nominations shall be void, and the expenses shall be paid by the subscribers, in proportion to the number of nominations taken by each. In the case of produce stakes, however, the original entries shall contine binding if the meeting is held at a later period of the season.

16. *Running in Order.*—Every dog must be brought up in its proper turn, without delay, under a penalty of £1. If absent for more than a quarter of an hour its opponent shall be entitled to claim the trial—and shall, in that case, run a bye. If both dogs be absent at the expiration of a quarter of an hour, the judge or judges shall have the power to disqualify both dogs, or to fine their owners any sum not exceeding £5 each.

17. *By whom a Dog is to be Hunted.*—An owner, his keeper, or deputy may hunt a dog, but it must be one or the other ; and, when once the dogs are down, an owner must not interfere with his dog if he has deputed another person to hunt him.

18. *Method of Hunting.*—The person hunting a dog may speak, whistle, and work him by hand, as he thinks proper ; but he can be called to order by the judges for making any unnecessary noise, and if he persists in doing so they can order the dog to be taken up, and he will be out of the stake. An opponent's dog may not be purposely interfered with or excited, or an appeal can be made to the judges ; and if the opponent's dog points game, the other dog is not to be drawn across him to take the point, but if not backing of his own accord, he must be brought round behind the other dog. Dogs must be hunted together, and their keepers must walk within a reasonable distance of one another. After a caution, the judge or judges may have the power to disqualify the dog whose keeper persists in neglecting this rule.

19. *Control of Dogs Competing.*—The control of all matters connected with the dogs under trial shall rest with the judge or judges of the meeting, assisted in cases of peculiar difficulties by the stewards.

20. *Wearing Collars.*—All dogs, when necessary, shall wear collars—the red for the highest dog on the card, whose place shall be on the left, the white for the lowest dog, whose place shall be on the right side.

21. *The Judge or Judges.*—The judge or judges shall be subject to the general rules which may be established by the Kennel Club for his or their guidance. At the termination of each trial, he or they shall immediately proclaim his or their decision, either by word of mouth, or by the exhibition of a colour corresponding with that worn by the winning dog. No recalling or reversing of that decision shall be afterwards given on any pretext whatever.

22. *Length of Trials.*—The length of a trial shall be determined by the judge or judges. When he or they are satisfied that decided superiority has been exhibited by one of the contending dogs the trial should end.

23. *Injuring a Dog.*—If any subscriber or his servant shall, wilfully or by carelessness, injure, or cause to be injured, an opponent's dog during a trial, the owner of the dog so injured shall (although the trial be given against him) be deemed the winner of it, or shall have the option of allowing the other dog to remain and run out the stake, and in such case shall be entitled to half its winnings, if any.

24. *"No Trials" and "Undecideds."*—A "no-trial" is when, by accident or some other unforeseen cause, the dogs are not tried together. An "undecided" trial is where the judge or judges consider the merit of the dogs equal. If either is then drawn the owners must at the time declare which dog remains in. A "no-trial" or an "undecided" may be run again immediately, or at such a time during the meeting as the judge or judges may direct. If it stand over until the next day it shall be the first trial run.

25. *Withdrawal of Dog.*—If a dog be withdrawn from a stake on the field, its owner, or some one having his authority, must at once give notice to the secretary or stewards. If the dog belong to either of these officials, the notice must be given to one of the others.

26. *Impugning the Judge.*—If any subscriber openly impugns the decision of the judge or judges on the ground, he shall forfeit not more than £5, or less than £2, at the discretion of the majority of the stewards.

27. *Stakes not Run Out, and Arrangements Made Thereon.*—When two dogs remain in for the deciding trial, the stakes shall be considered divided if they belong to the same owner, or to confederates ; and also if the owner of one of the two dogs induces the owner of the other to draw him for any consideration ; but if one of the two be drawn without consideration (from lameness, injury, or from any cause clearly affecting his chance of winning), the other may be declared the winner, the facts of the case being clearly proved to the satisfaction of the stewards. The same rule shall apply when more than two dogs remain in at the end of a stake which is not run out ; and in case of a division between three or more dogs, of which two or more belonging to the same owner, these latter shall be held to take equal shares of the total amount received by their owner in the division. The terms

of any arrangement to divide winnings, and the amount of any money given to induce the owner of a dog to draw him, must be declared to the secretary.

28. *Objections.*—An objection to a dog may be made to the secretary or to any one of the stewards of a meeting at any time within ten days of the last day of the meeting, upon the objector lodging in the hands of such steward or secretary the sum of £5, which shall be forfeited if the objection prove frivolous, or if he shall not bring the case before the next meeting of the Kennel Club Committee, or give notice to the secretary previous thereto of his intention to withdraw the objection. The owner of the dog objected to must deposit equally the sum of £5, and prove the correctness of his entry or case. All expenses in consequence of the objection shall be borne by the party against whom the decision is given. Should an objection be made which cannot at the time be substantiated or disproved, the dog may be allowed to compete under protest, the secretary or stewards retaining his winnings until the objection has been withdrawn, or heard and decided. If the dog objected to be disqualified, the amount to which he would otherwise have been entitled shall be divided equally among the dogs beaten by him, and if a piece of plate or prize has been added and won by him, only the dogs which he beat in the several rounds shall have a right to contend for it.

29. *Defaulters.*—No person shall be allowed to enter or run a dog in his own or any other person's name who is a defaulter for either stakes, forfeits, or bets in connection with field trials or dog shows, or for any money due under an arrangement for a division of winnings, or for penalties regularly imposed for the infraction of rules by the stewards of any meeting, or for any payment required by a decision of the Kennel Club, or for subscriptions due to any club entitled to acknowledgment by the Kennel Club. As regards bets, however, this rule shall only apply when a complaint is lodged with the secretary of the Kennel Club within six months after the bet becomes due. On receipt of such complaint the secretary shall give notice of the claim to the person against whom it is made, with a copy of this rule, and if he shall not pay the bet or appear before the next meeting of the Kennel Club and resist the claim successfully, he shall be considered a defaulter.

30. *Ineligible Persons.*—Any person who is proved to the satisfaction of the Kennel Club Committee to have been guilty of any fraudulent or discreditable conduct in connection with dogs, may, in addition to any pecuniary penalty to which he may be liable, be declared incapable of entering a dog in his own or any other person's name during any subsequent period that the club may decide upon.

31. *Unfitness to Compete.*—Should any dog be considered by the judges of a meeting unfit to compete by reason of being on "heat," or having any contagious disease, or any other cause which clearly interferes with the safety or chance of winning of his opponent, such dog shall be disqualified.

N.B.—In the foregoing rules the term "dog" is understoood to mean both sexes.

We are decidedly of the opinion that Field Trials have done much towards the improvement of sporting dogs, and hope to see them more extensively held all over the country. They have in some degree, if not perfectly, the merit of combining the element of public competition with those practical tests so desirable in judging of sporting dogs. In these field trials the Setters have hitherto managed to hold their own uncommonly well, and up to the year 1880 no Pointer has succeeded in winning the Grand Challenge Cup which is given by the Kennel Club to be run for annually by dogs belonging to its members. Any member may run any dog he chooses, either Pointer or Setter, and it was decided when the cup was first offered that it should become the property of any member who should be fortunate enough to win it three times, but not necessarily in succession or with the same dog. To the astonishment of the sporting world Mr. G. De Landre Macdona has accomplished the feat with Ranger, a black-and-white Setter, whose portrait and pedigree we give on the following pages. This grand dog, though not himself a perfect model of beauty, has by carrying off the Challenge Cup upon three occasions stamped himself as the Setter of the day, and has moreover shown what is behind him in the matter of pedigree by begetting many first-class specimens of the breed. As a matter of fact Ranger III., who is the subject of our coloured plate, is himself a grandson of the old dog, and we therefore add his pedigree to the table, as Ranger's is naturally included in it:—

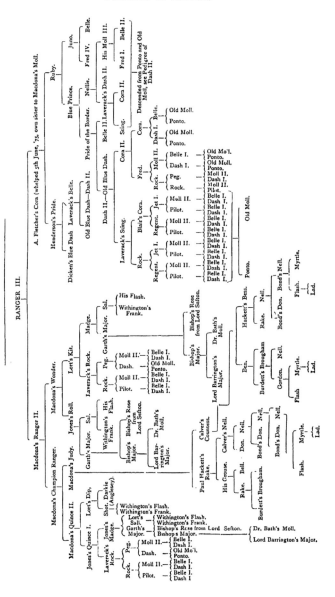

PEDIGREE OF MR. G. DE LANDRE MACDONA'S ENGLISH SETTER DOG, RANGER III.

Whelped 8th March, 1877.

27

With reference to Ranger's marvellous behaviour in the field we extract the following from a report of the Field Trials which appeared in the *Live Stock Journal*, April 25th, 1879. In alluding to Ranger the writer says:—

"He made what is so much to the public taste at these trials—a sensation point. When running down a large grass meadow with Darkie he rushed with marvellous speed to the bottom, against which appeared a large embankment. The dog suddenly found

MR. MACDONA'S CHAMPION ENGLISH SETTER "RANGER."

himself hurled by the impetus of his going into the midst of a twelve-foot river that ran between the embankment and the grass field in which he was running. The impetus with which he went threw him to the opposite side. Crawling up the bank half dazed with the shock, he scented some birds, and immediately coming to life again, dropped. The birds then rising, he plunged back into the river, swam across, and shook himself in face of the judges and spectators. Anything more unique or sensational in the matter of field trials has not been witnessed before, except when he won the all-aged stake at the Kennel Club Field Trials, when, rushing down the hill, he suddenly winded birds, and stopped, and the impetus of his going caused him to make a summersault in the air, when he landed on his back, and as stiff as starch. His four legs were seen in the air, and his neck and head turned round in the direction where the birds were soon put up about a foot from his nose."

ENGLISH SETTER.

Ranger, in addition to his Challenge Cup triumphs, has won the following stakes :—Reynold Stakes, Shrewsbury, 1874 ; Champion Cup, Shrewsbury, 1874; Champion Cup, Shrewsbury, 1877 ; Shrewsbury Stakes, 1877 ; Hawkstone Stakes, Shrewsbury, 1873 ; East of England Stakes, Ipswich, 1873 ; Trehill Stakes, Devon and Cornwall, 1875. Such performances, even unaccompanied by the fact that he has won the Challenge Cup outright, stamp Ranger as undoubtedly the best dog of his breed which has hitherto appeared.

To recommend the Setter as a companion dog to the non-sporting philo-kuon may be to invite a sneer from many a knight of the trigger, but nevertheless there is much to be said in favour of these dogs in the character of mere companions. There is no more elegant dog than the Setter ; the outlines of a well-formed specimen are eminently beautiful, and his every movement most graceful. The coat is beautifully soft and rich, the featherings especially being of a fine silky texture, and the colours and distribution of them generally striking and picturesque, as they are soft, refined, and lovely. In intelligence the Setter has few equals, so that he soon accommodates himself to circumstances, and is so easy of control that he readily becomes a companion that can be thoroughly trusted, for his intelligence is great, and he seems to think for himself, and make the pleasing of his owner his sole delight. In temper they are almost invariably reliable, and their affections become deep and lasting. And added to all these qualities there is an air of refinement and superiority about him, inherited from a long line of blue-blooded ancestors, that commends him to all.

Those who keep but a few Setters to shoot over themselves should never fail to make friends and constant companions of them ; the mutual understanding and trust arising from this doubles the pleasure of the sportsman in the possession of his dogs, and adds greatly to his success in the field.

We had Mr. Macdona's Ranger with us whilst Mr. Barber was sketching him, and although we met as strangers we were soon friends, and parted we firmly believe with mutual regret. Never have we seen a dog who so readily accommodated himself to circumstances—he seemed at once to be as much at home in London as he is in the stubble or the heather, and took his seat in a hansom cab as naturally as though to the manner born.

One word of caution only in respect to keeping Setters as companions. We should always advise having them broken to game, although there may be no prospect of using them ; because if unbroken dogs were bred from an unbroken line, whilst their beauty and general intelligence might be sustained, they would lose the aptitude for their natural work.

As stated at the commencement of this article, it is an unquestionable fact that, whatever the source was from which the modern English Setter sprung, there are several distinct families of the breed at present in existence. But even these are themselves offshoots of older types, which in their turn originated from the Setting dog, either by breeding and selection, or the judicious admixture of foreign blood. It may therefore be as well to draw attention to some of the most famous of the old breeds, as well as make allusion to the most fashionable of the modern ones, before proceeding further with the subject.

Reference has already been made to the old *Welsh Setter*, a breed now practically extinct, and whose loss is so greatly to be deplored that supreme efforts should be made to restore it, before all hopes of doing so are vain. Mr. William Lort, of Fron Goch Hall, Montgomeryshire, who has before been quoted in this chapter, has kindly given us some valuable information concerning this variety of Setter, which is in purport as follows :—The coat of

30

the Welsh or Llanidloes Setter, or at all events of pure-bred ones, is as curly as the jacket of a Cotswold sheep, and, not only is it curly, but it is hard in texture, and as unlike that of a modern fashionable Setter as it is possible to imagine. The colour is usually white, with occasionally a lemon-coloured patch or two about the head and ears. Many, however, are pure white, and it is unusual not to find several whelps in every litter possessed of one or two pearl eyes. Their heads are longer in proportion to their size, and not so refined-looking as those of the English Setter. Sterns are curly and clubbed, with no fringe on them, and the tail swells out in shape something like an otter's. This breed is more useful than any Spaniel, for it is smart, handy, with an excellent nose, and can find with tolerable certainty at the moderate pace it goes. It usually has the habit of beating close to you, and is not too fast, being particularly clever at cocks and snipe, which they are no more likely to miss than is a Spaniel. With so much to recommend them, we cannot help repeating that this is a breed well worth saving from extinction, especially as it is so hardy, and far less liable to disease than the modern fashionable dog. Some excellent specimens of this variety have been in the hands of Mr. Charles Beck, of Upton Priory, Macclesfield, and he said that they stood hard work and briary dingles, when he worked them in Wales, better than any breed he could procure.

There was also a *liver-and-white* strain of Setter which was well known in the North of England, especially in the Carlisle district. Though this dog was coarse and lumbering, it has been argued, and as often denied, that the famous Laverack blood is tinged with that of this variety. However, this will be more fully referred to almost immediately, when the Laveracks are touched upon.

Another famous strain of jet-black Welsh Setters is now lost and gone for ever. It was a blood that was to be found in many parts of the Principality, and as a strain was second to none. Unfortunately, though jealously guarded by its owners, their interest in it gradually lessened, and it finally has disappeared entirely.

The *Anglesea Setter*, as it was once called, did not spring, as might be supposed, from the island of that name, but from Beaudesert, the residence of the Marquis of Anglesea, where it was carefully treasured. They were in character a light, active, very narrow breed of dog, with no chest, though deep in ribs. They were rather leggy, and possessed the habit of standing with their fore-legs and feet close together. This breed of dog was constitutionally delicate, but as long as they stayed, showed great pace in the field. In colour they were mostly black - white - and - tan, and in coat, though not so smooth and flat as a modern Setter, the Angleseas were not nearly so curly as the Welshmen described above.

To arrive more rapidly at the leading strains in 1880, we now come to the magic name of Edward Laverack, a gentleman who has done more to bring this Setter in all his glory before the public than any other has ever done or is likely to do. Mr. Laverack, who was an ardent sportsman, for half a century was engaged in improving the English Setter, and with most flattering results. The corner-stone of his breeding-stud was a pair he first obtained from a clergyman named Harrison, who resided in the neighbourhood of Carlisle. That he conscientiously followed the principles of strict in-breeding is amply proved by a reference to the pedigree table of Ranger, where it will be observed that all Mr. Laverack's best blood is represented on the one side ; and the success of his system is clearly demonstrated by the position his strain occupies in the estimation of modern Setter breeders. In short, most of the leading strains are either pure Laveracks, or else they partake largely

31

of the Laverack blood. The formation of the Laverack Setter, to quote his own words, is as follows :—

"Head long and light, not snake-headed or deep flewed, but a sufficiency of lip; remarkable for being very strong in the fore-quarters; chest, deep, *wide*, and ribs well sprung behind the shoulders, carrying the breadth of back to where the tail is set on; immensely strong across the loins; shoulders very slanting or oblique; particularly short from the shoulders to where the hind-quarters meet. A Setter should not rise or be too upright in the shoulder, but *level* and *broad*; tail well set on in a line with the back, *rather drooping*, scimitar-shaped, and with plenty of flag. Legs remarkably short, and very short from hock to foot; feet close and compact, thighs particularly well bent or crooked, well placed and close under the body of the animal, not wide or straggling.

"Colour black, or blue-and-white ticked; coat, long, soft, and silky in texture; eyes, soft, mild, and intelligent, of a dark hazel colour; ears low set on and close to the head, giving a round development to the skull. There is another variety of the same strain called the lemon-and-white Beltons, exactly the same breed and blood. These are marked similar to the Blues, except being spotted all through with lemon-colour instead of blue, and precisely of the same form and characteristics; equally good, hardy, and enduring."

These words of Mr. Edward Laverack must surely be treasured by Setter breeders, and the only unsatisfactory part in them to our mind is the total absence of any allusion to liver-colour. We cannot see how he can reconcile himself to ignore all reference to, this liver-colour, since, in the following letter to Mr. Rothwell, an old friend and fellow-breeder, he distinctly admits that there is a strong dash of liver blood in the Laverack Setter. The letter referred to runs as follows :—

[Copy.]

"Broughall Cottage,
"Whitchurch,
"Shropshire

"Dear Rothwell,

"I am glad to hear your bitch has given birth; save me a Blue. All five are true bred, and all take after the sire, Blue Prince. The liver-and-white will be quite as handsome and good as any. He strains to Prince's sire, viz., Pride of the Border, a liver-and-white; he strains back for thirty years to a change of blood I once introduced—the pure old Edward Castle breed—County Cumberland liver-and-white, quite as pure and as good as the Blues. You may have heard Withington speak of the handsomest Setter he ever saw, viz., Pilot; he was this colour, and a clipper. Pride's dam was my old blue-and-white, with tan cheeks and eyebrows. Why I reserved Pride was to breed back with him and my Blues. He is invaluable, as by him I can carry on the breed. . . . . . I have a demand from America for more than I can sell, but they are the best, and I *guarantee* all I send *bred* by *me*. . . . . . .

"Yours truly,
"E. Laverack.

"*May 23rd, 1874.*"

There is a possibility that Mr. Laverack, knowingly or otherwise, had introduced some of the blood of the liver-coloured Setters we have above alluded to as being in the neighbourhood of Carlisle. This breed was not a popular one, we understand, and therefore it might not have been worth his while to make a special reference to it. But be this as it may, one thing is very evident from the letter, and that is that Mr. Rothwell, who bred many dogs for Mr. Laverack himself, was unaware of any such a taint, or this letter would not have been written. Its present publication may be a consolation to breeders of this kind of dog, as the appearance of a liver-coloured whelp will convince an owner who has read these lines that it is not necessarily a bar-sinister in the pureness of its pedigree as a Laverack. There could in fact be a great deal said upon this subject of the liver colour, which Mr. Laverack here remarks upon as being likely to appear now and then in pure-bred dogs of his strain. A tendency to throw back is of course inevitable in every breed of animal, and it is greatly to be regretted that in his work Mr. Laverack threw no light upon the origin of his breed. In fact, in his description of the Setter, he only alludes, in referring to his own strain, to black, or blue, and lemon-ticked ones. This reticence on the part of Mr. Laverack would seem to imply that, though he did not attempt to deny the fact that there was liver blood somewhere in his strain, he was not particularly anxious that this should be generally known, and consequently kept even his *fidus achates*, Mr. Rothwell, in the dark about it until some puppies of the colour appeared in his breeding operations, when he hastened to assure the latter gentleman that such an event was by no means impossible.

It would appear, further, not only from the above letter, but from many others which passed between Messrs. Laverack and Rothwell, and which subsequently came into our hands, that the latter gentleman, who appears to have had the free use of any of Mr. Laverack's stud dogs, was in the habit of giving Mr. Laverack puppies as the latter required them ; and also that the great breeder himself was kind enough to sell Miss Rothwell's whelps for her. We do not consider ourselves that there is any harm in such a thing being done; but the practice is unfortunate, inasmuch as it opens the door to ill-natured remarks on the pedigrees of dogs, and is a practical illustration of the dangers to which breeders are liable. What we particularly allude to is the chance that is run of the authenticity of pedigrees being disputed afterwards, if it could be proved that certain dogs were actually bred by Mr. Rothwell, and not by Mr. Laverack. We do not impute any deception to either of these gentlemen, but it is possible that persons who purchased pure-bred Laveracks from himself might describe them as bred by him, when in reality Mr. Rothwell deserved the honour.

Another and generally unknown fact in connection with the English Setter-breeding operations of Mr. Edward Laverack is beyond a doubt ; and that is, that in the year 1874 he was practically "out of" his own blood. Whether the fatalities to which he so pathetically refers in the following correspondence were in any way accelerated by the excess of in-breeding to which he had resorted we cannot say, but it would seem that for some years his stock had been dying off in a manner which was surprising to the great breeder himself, and caused him to draw upon the kennel of his friend Mr. Rothwell for dogs to supply his customers. The following extracts from some of Mr. Laverack's letters may be read with interest :—

"Broughall Cottage,
"Whitchurch,
"Salop.

"DEAR ROTHWELL,

"I received your daughter's letter relative to the puppies. When old enough to take from mamma, place in a hamper, and send as directed above, and *advise* me *prior* in order I may send to station for them. Keep them till six weeks old. I shall be able to sell your daughter as many as you can spare ; and when sold, will send either you or Miss Rothwell the money. . . . . .

"Yours truly,
"E. LAVERACK.

"*June 17th*, 1874."

"Broughall Cottage,
"Whitchurch,
"Salop.

"DEAR MR. ROTHWELL,

"I regret very much to inform you the three puppies you sent died a week ago in distemper, after rearing them all straight, and they really became beautiful, and showed a deal of quality. They were all three *bespoke* by an *American* at 15 guineas, to be sent in March. But what is still worse, I have lost *six more* dogs, *two brood* bitches 18 months old, which I refused to sell at fifty guineas apiece, and *four* more young dogs, all cut off in *distemper and fits.* All were the handsomest I ever bred or saw. Indeed, I am quite broken in spirits to think after all my trouble and expense (a life's), I fear I have or shall lose the breed, as I have only one old brood bitch left, I fear too old to breed. The only dog I have left except her is Prince. . . . . .

"Yours very truly,
"E. LAVERACK."

There is no date to the above letter, but the post-mark on the envelope is November 13th, 1874.

"Broughall,
"Whitchurch,
"Salop.

"DEAR ROTHWELL,

". . . . . . I am quite disheartened with the loss I have sustained—*nine.* Six were such as I never saw for beauty, and the three that came from you had greatly improved. I have only two old dogs left—viz., Prince and a lemon bitch, Cora. I have been here three years and only reared one dog out of 30. As I took this place apparently everything I could wish, and built an excellent kennel, and have a free range of fields, my dogs being cut off seems a fatality, as no expense is spared. . . . . . I will bring over several letters from America relative to dogs, and I think if I approve of your young ones I may perhaps get you a customer. . . . . .

"Yours most truly,
"E. LAVERACK.

"*March 24th,* 1875."

. Such letters clearly show the difficulties under which Mr. Laverack laboured at the close of his career, and have no doubt been instrumental in earning the pure-bred Laverack Setter a reputation in certain quarters for being delicate and hard to rear. On the other hand, the success of crossing the Laverack blood with other strains is proved by the success of Ranger; and in our opinion there is a great probability of the English Setter deteriorating if modern breeders stick too closely to their own blood.

Amongst the number of great Setter breeders may be mentioned those of George Jones of Oscott, who was a great light at the first institution of dog shows, and showed Rap. Mr. Jones gloried in the Laverack blood, which he grafted on his own stock, and cheerfully acknowledged the benefits he received from it. The Brothers Withington, too, were great Setter men, and good friends to Mr. Laverack. They are said to have given the latter one hundred pounds for four unbroken puppies, which was then a very long price to give for dogs of such a tender age. Nor must the names of G. R. Rogerson and the Rev. Francis Adey be forgotten by lovers of the Setter. Mr. Statter, too, will always be remembered in connection with this breed. His great kennel is very near the top of the tree in Setter circles, and though its members are not all pure Laveracks, their owner sensibly admits that the more of this blood he gets the better pleased he is. Mr. R. Ll. Purcell-Llewellin, of Lincolnshire, is one of the greatest Laverack breeders of the day, and spares no trouble or expense in perfecting his strain. In consequence he has many grand specimens, though many breeders say that his bitches are better than his dogs. Lord Waterpark's handsome, heavily-flecked Setters, which appeared at a very early Glasgow dog-show, were, and have been, much admired. They are believed by many to be closely allied in blood to the original Laveracks, and their appearance certainly justifies the supposition.

The kennel of Mr. William Lort, now of Fron Goch Hall, Llanllugan, Montgomeryshire, is also one which must always be regarded with respect. To quote the words of Mr. Laverack himself:—

" Mr. Lort has also a beautiful and excellent breed of Setters, descended principally from the strain of the late Richard Withington, Ashfield House, Pendleton, Manchester, an old friend of mine, and who shot with me for many years in the Highlands. They are black-and-white and lemon-and-white; long, silky coats, hard enduring, and good rangers.

" Mr. Lort, from judging so constantly at dog shows, has given this fine strain but little chance, and they are not known as they ought to be; but from what I am told, and believe to be the case, there are no *better* . . . Setter breeders are under the greatest obligations to this gentleman for his unflagging endeavours to improve the Setter, and he spares no time, trouble, or expense."

Such praise from one who, like Mr. Edward Laverack, is the recognised father of the modern Setter, is a sufficient guarantee for the quality of Mr. Lort's strain, whilst his popularity as *facile princeps* the leading Setter authority now alive, is quite beyond a doubt. Mr. T. B. Bowers, of Woolton, near Liverpool, is also a noted Setter breeder, and glories in his admiration of the Laverack blood. Mr. John Shorthose, of Newcastle, whose grand bitch Novel is illustrated in this chapter, has several good specimens of the breed, and is a successful exhibitor at most of the leading shows. The great Shropshire kennel of Mr. Daintry Collins contains some of the best blood we have, being mostly pure-bred Laveracks. Sir Frederick Graham, too, has made his mark as a successful breeder; and both Lord Down and Mr. Barclay Field have been fortunate to produce successful Field Trial winners. Nor can the name of Mr. George Lowe's Tam o' Shanter be omitted from any list of the leading Setters and sires of the day.

Amongst the most prominent Setters of recent years the name of Rap will always be conspicuous. We believe that this dog was beaten in his day by Mr. Laverack's Prince, but he is generally credited with having been the best dog of the breed ever seen in public. A gentleman who knew him well when in his prime has kindly given us the following description of this great English Setter :—" Rap was a black-white-and-tan dog, with a most refined head, and very intelligent eyes. His ears were beautifully placed, and his long neck was well set into his back. His ribs were deep, his feet were good, and his legs as straight as gun-barrels ; his hind-quarters were powerful ; and last, but not least by any means, he had a well-carried, well-proportioned stern. His single fault, if fault there could be found in Rap, was that he was a trifle—just a trifle—high on his leg."

Mr. William Lort's Shot (1865) was another famous pure Laverack, and own brother to Sal, who was pronounced by Mr. Richard Withington to be the best bitch of the day. Mr. Laverack, however, who never saw either Shot or Sal, said Walter was the best Setter he had ever seen ; they were by Withington's Frank, out of Flash. Nor must the merits of Quince II., Ranger's father, be overlooked, unlucky as this grand dog was in his owners, for he never seemed to be properly appreciated by those who had him in their possession. Quince II.

was sold for a few shillings, when worn out, at Aldridge's Repository in 1878, for the public never seemed to realise that very likely much of Ranger's excellence was inherited from his brave old sire. Count Wind'em, Countess Moll, and Countess Bear, are the bright particular stars of Mr. Llewellin's kennel, and the first-named is a great, big, useful-looking dog. Mr. James Fletcher's blue-ticked dog Rock, late Mr. S. E. Shirley's, has done a lot of winning, and Mr. Lort's own brother to him—Jock—is a successful sire, having fathered Belfast and other good ones. Milano, a black-tan-and-white (very little tan-and-white) dog, and Bandit, have done much to sustain the prestige of Mr. Bowers' kennel, and Mr. Shorthose's Novel has kept his name well before the public. Another English Setter who is, in our opinion, a very grand but unlucky dog, is Mr. J. Robinson's Emperor Fred; his chief fault is a want of spring in the ribs, but, with this exception, he is a Setter all over. Mr. T. B. Bowers, in addition to Bandit, is the fortunate possessor of an excellent bitch in Maid of Honour, who closely resembles the great dog in both colour and formation.

Having thus endeavoured to trace out the history of the English Setter from its earliest origin until the present day, and having drawn attention to many of the men who have done best for it, and many of the dogs who have done most to support the English Setter's reputation, there remains for us but very little more to say. Opinions on the Setter's merits must always be re-occurring when the large number of sportsmen is taken into consideration; and even in former days, as we have already shown, it was a debatable subject in sporting circles as to which was the better dog in the field—the Setter or the Pointer. For our own part we should prefer the Setter, but a good dog, like a good horse, is good under any circumstances. Mr. William Lort, in answer to a question, has written us as follows:—"I am often asked which is the better dog—the Pointer or the Setter. It is difficult to say. I keep and use both, and the only disadvantage I see in the Pointer is that on high, storm-swept hills he does sometimes, after a protracted lunch, shiver and shut up; but this is only on exceptionally wet and cold days. The Setter is undoubtedly the best dog we have for grouse-shooting, and this is beyond a doubt the poetry of all shooting.

"Now, as to the points of the English Setter, it is really difficult to give them in an understandable form—general appearance, or *tout ensemble*, goes for so much. The head ought to be long, and the eyes, which should match or be in keeping with the colour or complexion of the dog, should not be too wide apart, or placed in too deep a stop, or be separated by too much of a groove—all or any of these defects spoil the expression, a most important point in a Setter. The ears should not be set on too high or be carried too far from the head. The front part of the ear should not gape open so as to show the inside of the ear. The ear should not be Spaniel-like and large. The neck should be long and well set back into the shoulders. The chest should be deep, and the ribs carried well back towards the hips. N.B.—Some loose-loined, badly ribbed-up Setters go a great pace, but they are usually bad feeders, and not every-day workers. The stern should not be too long; it should be carried in a line with the back, and be straight, and be ornamented with a little pendant fringe. Nothing indicates mongrel blood in a Setter more than a defective stern. The forelegs should be straight, strong, and not too long; the hind ones should be muscular and well-bent. The feet should be round, and well supplied with hair between toes, not too far apart. The coat is affected by climate; the most approved is devoid of curl. The best colours are black-and-white, ticked, or blue Beltons, lemon-and-white, and lemon-ticked. Laverack preferred the blue Beltons; he thought them rather hardier than dogs of other colours."

36

Having thus given the ideas of the leading living authority upon Setters it only remains for us to give a short description of the principal points of the variety. They are as follows:—

The *Head*, moderately long, and not too heavy; rather inclined to be narrow between the ears; a dip below the eyes, and with the muzzle rather up-rising at the nose.

The *Nose* should be large and the nostrils spreading; the colour, black or dark liver, dependent upon the colour of the dog himself.

The *Ears* not too heavy, set on low, and lying close to the head, not pricked up, and covered with a silky fringe.

MR. J. H. SHORTHOSE'S ENGLISH SETTER BITCH "NOVEL."

The *Eyes* large, bright, and intelligent; nothing is so bad as a "pig-eyed" Setter.

The *Neck* long, curved, sloping, and well set on to the shoulders.

The *Shoulders* very muscular, and sloped.

The *Chest* deep.

The *Body*. Ribs rather round, wide at the shoulders, well ribbed-up and muscular; loins a little arched.

The *Legs and Feet*. Legs not too long, *quite* straight, and feathered down to the ground; feet well supplied with hair. In hind legs the stifles must be well bent, and the hocks and pasterns unusually strong.

The *Stern or Flag* not too long, and free from curl, and carried in a slight curve; it should be well feathered.

The *Coat* is soft, silky, and free from all curl.

The *Colour*. Lemon-and-white, blue-and-white, orange-and-white, black-and-white, white, black, and liver-and-white. There are other colours, but they are seldom met with.

In *General Appearance* the Setter is a handsome though delicate-looking dog; in many instances increasing this appearance by a tendency to crouch and seem afraid. He, however, ought to give evidences of stamina, and should have a cut-and-come-again appearance in spite of seeming delicate.

The dog selected for illustration in our coloured plate is Mr. Macdona's Ranger III., a grandson of Old Ranger. This dog's pedigree has already been given, and, as he has been expatriated to Germany, it would be unfair to criticise his performances upon the bench.

The engravings of Ranger and Novel are, we consider, two excellent likenesses of the animals they represent. Ranger, also Mr. Macdona's, has already been done justice to above, and we can only add that he is as affectionate and obedient in private life as he is feared and formidable in the field. Mr. Shorthose's Novel was bred by Mr. T. B. Cockerton in 1877, and is by Blue Prince out of Flame, by Rall out of Countess, Blue Prince II. by Blue Prince out of Cora. She has won the following prizes:—Gateshead first and cup, Whitby first, Preston first, Kendal cup, Bishop Auckland champion, and Birmingham second prize, 1879; first Crystal Palace, first Darlington, 1880.

STANDARD OF POINTS FOR JUDGING ENGLISH SETTERS.

	Value.
Head	10
Eyes and ears	5
Shoulders and neck	5
Body and chest	10
Loins and stifles...	5
Legs and feet	5
Coat and feather	5
General appearance	5
Total	50

38

THE ENGLISH SETTER.

WITHOUT doubt, to the late Mr. Edward Laverack, who died in April, 1877, the present generation is indebted for the excellence of the setter, both in form and work, as he is found to-day, and, with few exceptions, the very best dogs are actual descendants of the Laverack strain. That there is, however, such a thing as a " pure Laverack " to be found now in 1892 I very much dispute. The best strains have a cross or two cropping in somewhere or other. Mr. R. L. Purcell Llewellin, to whom Mr. Laverack dedicated his volume on the setter, claims a strain of his own, which perhaps has been more successful than any other, both in the field and on the show bench. Mr. Llewellin has, however, kept it very much to himself, so the continuation of the general improvement, at any rate in appearance, of this dog, has been due to another source. This is from the kennel of Mr. James B. Cockerton, of

Ravensbarrow Lodge, North Lancashire, who, in reality, had his first setter from Mr. Laverack.

It appears that some forty-five years or more ago, the author of " The Setter " was in the habit of going into the neighbourhood of Mr. Cockerton's residence to shoot during September, and he left behind him, with the uncle of the latter (Mr. Myles Birket, Birket Houses, Winster), one or two setters, from which the present strain has, with the aid of slight infusions of other strains, been continued with extraordinary success. Thus they are more or less inter-bred, and resist very much the introduction of new blood. This, Mr. Cockerton has repeatedly found to be the case, he having on several occasions introduced a fresh strain by the purchase of a stud dog. In no instance has the progeny answered expectations. They were destroyed, and their sire came to a similar end. Later he tried a well-known field trial winner, Dr. Wood's Fred W., of great excellence in the field, and by no means indifferent in appearance. The result, however, did not turn out any more satisfactorily than previous off-crosses had done.

However, to the origin of the " Laveracks." We are told that Mr. Laverack first obtained his strain from the Rev. A. Harrison, who resided near Carlisle, and he informs us in his book, published in 1872 when he was seventy-three years of age, that he had been breeding setters for fifty years. His first fancy for them must have been well on to seventy years ago. At that time, and for long after, the pedigrees of dogs were of little value, and, so long as the strain was good for work, and not bad to look at, people did not care a jot what the blood was. Mr. Laverack, however, had found that he could, by a few generations of judicious crossing, breed setters more true to type than others had done.

He was a sportsman, spent most of his time in shooting and in sub-letting shootings, travelled much in Scotland and the North of England, and so became acquainted with the various strains of setters then extant. Two or three years before his death the present writer repeatedly met Mr. Laverack, and a mutual admiration of the dog led to a considerable interchange of ideas on the subject, and on setters in particular. Although he would never acknowledge any cross from the original Old Moll and Ponto, which he had obtained from Mr. Harrison in 1825, I am not quite certain such was not tried. There were strains in the North of England that he valued highly, and which, no doubt, he would find useful for the purpose of putting vigour and size into his puppies, for it is a little against nature to produce in so short a time such good dogs as he owned by breeding from brothers and sisters, as he did with Dash I. and Belle—the one a black and white, the other an orange and white. However, the pedigrees of Dash II. and Moll III.—the latter black, white, and tan, both great, great grandchildren of the original brace—are fully set out in his book, and, of course, cannot be gainsaid. It is, however, strange that the black, tan, and whites, and the liver and whites, of the same "pure" strains did not come out until the later generations, nor, until actually pressed upon the point, did he acknowledge that a liver and white puppy was the genuine article.

His friend Rothwell, who had the use of the best Laveracks for breeding purposes, wrote him that one of his puppies was liver and white. To this a reply came to the effect that it was all right, and that the colour came back from a strain of the "Edmond Castle" breed, Cumberland, which he had introduced about thirty years before! Rather a peculiar period for a cross to remain in abeyance before it came out, and which no scientist would believe possible. It is extremely likely that, up to a comparatively late date, Mr. Laverack crossed with the Cumberland and Northumberland dogs, most of which were liver and white; and so we have that colour in the setter to this day, and there it will remain. Twenty years or more ago I saw several of these liver and white dogs that had more than a tendency to the top knot, which was a prevailing feature with the Naworth Castle strain, and in another which the late Major Cowen kept at Blaydon Burn, near Newcastle-on-Tyne.

Whatever crosses may have been used by Mr Laverack, or by his friends, there is no doubt that such proved extremely useful, and have been the means of fully establishing the strain on a sound and substantial basis. In his own kennel, towards the close of his career, Mr. Laverack was not fortunate in rearing his puppies, and at the time of his death there were but five setters in his actual possession. These were Blue Prince, Blue Rock, Cora (lemon and white), Blue Belle, and Nellie or Blue Cora. The two latter were own sisters, and Mr. Laverack's housekeeper sold Prince, Belle, and another to Mr. T. B. Bowers for about 100*l*. The remaining brace ultimately went to Mr. J. R. Robinson, of Sunderland, who held a kind of partnership with the late Mr. Laverack, and had laid claim to the whole of the kennel; but the three dogs Mr. Bowers bought were sold even before poor Laverack was laid in his grave near the quiet little church at Ash, not far from Whitchurch. The Kennel Club Stud Books tell us how the blood of these setters has been disseminated since that time.

Mr. Laverack claimed for his dogs excellence all round in the field, and unusual stamina; indeed, he talked to me of working them ten, twelve, and fourteen hours a day for a fortnight. That they were good dogs goes without saying; but " Stonehenge " did not care about their work in the early days of Field Trials, for he said they had not good noses, carried their heads low, and were lacking that fine tail action that he so much valued either in pointer or setter.

As a show dog, Mr. Laverack's Dash II., better known, perhaps, as old Blue Dash, was a typical specimen; and from, say, 1869 to 1872, was, perhaps, the best setter appearing on the bench. He had size bone, coat, and general symmetry to commend him, though his shoulders were rather upright and his neck not quite of the best, whilst his appearance would certainly have been smarter had he been cleaner cut under the throat. He was good enough to win at Birmingham, the Crystal Palace, and else-where, and in looks was far the best dog that I ever saw in his owner's possession. Another beautiful setter of Laverack's early strain was Mr. Dickon's Belle, and, it was said, equally excellent in the field and the show ring. So far as field trial dogs are concerned, Mr. Laverack mentions Mr. Garth's Daisy and Mr. Purcell Llewellin's Countess as the best ; but, although both were fast, very fast, the one had but a moderate nose and the other was said to be somewhat addicted to false pointing. Both were alluded to in the reports of the trials where they competed as possessing the above faults, which Mr. J. H. Walsh considered to arise from in-breeding.

Allusion must be made to Mr. Llewellin's Dan, Novel, Bondhu, Dash III., Count Wind'em ; and Mr. Field's Bruce, and to Lord Downe's Sam, who also went into the Llewellin kennels ; Armstrong's Old Kate was extremely useful as a brood bitch to that family of skilled dog trainers ; to Mr. S. E. Shirley's Rock, who, perhaps, won more bench prizes than any other setter ; to Mr. Barclay Field's Duke, a great field trial winner in 1866 and 1867 ; to Mr. T. B. Bowers' Frank, the handsomest orange and white setter of that time ; to Mr. Armstrong's Dash, sold to Mr. Brewis, Mr. G. Lowes' Tam o' Shanter ; Mr. T. Cunnington's Sir Alister ; and many other celebrities in their day might likewise be mentioned. Mr. Llewellin purchased Dan from Mr. T. Statter at the Shrewsbury trials in 1871, where he won the two stakes in which he competed and the extra prize for the best dog at that gathering. Dan owing to dislocating his shoulders never appeared in public afterwards but proved extremely useful in the kennel which so long remained his home.

Some of these improved Laveracks are not now so successful at the field trial meetings as they ought to be; but whether this arises rather from the lack of opportunity or from other causes it is difficult to say. As a fact, those persons who own the handsome dogs, mostly of the Laverack strain, that win on the show bench, do not, as a rule, train them for field trial work. This has been noticed to such an extent as to draw forth the remark that the field trial dog and the show dog are two distinct articles. I am of opinion that the absence of the show dog from the public field arises from the fact that he has not been afforded training opportunities and not from natural unfitness. Of course there are good and bad dogs of all strains, and it is not every dog, even from the best of parents that ever worked at a trial, that will come forward creditably in a similar position, and I am certain that, did Mr. Cockerton, already alluded to, enter his dogs for field trial work as Mr. Llewellin and others do theirs, the former would give quite as good an account of themselves as the others.

Monk of Furness, one of the show strain and a bench champion, was as good a dog in the field as ever ran, and at times, says Nicholson, who trained him at Ercall Heath, near Market Drayton, had done better work than any other in his kennel. He performed creditably at the National Trials, though it was not one of his best days. He, however, was the sire of Mr. Nicholson's Master Sam, Mr. F. Lowe's little bitch, Nun of Kippen, and Mr. T. Lauder's Sweep the Green, whose public work was quite as good as any one need wish to see. Monk of Furness was sold to go to Canada for 230*l*.

Few of these show dogs are, as I have hinted, put into proper hands to bring out their working powers, hence, what may be called, the cross-bred dogs do best. Of these, the liver and whites appear to excel all others, especially some of those that had Baron Doveridge for sire. He was bred by Lord Waterpark, was by Fred V. from Rue by Drake—Rival; Fred, by Blue Prince—Dicken's Belle; thus combining two distinct strains.

These are by no means handsome dogs, but they never appear to tire, have good noses, and are always on the look out for game. The late Mr. Heywood-Lonsdale's Woodhill Bruce and his sister Woodhill Beta I have seen run trials that could not well have been excelled; and both Mr. F. Lowe and Mr. F. Warde have had liver and white dogs of the same strains that did excellent work, Trip of Kippen not only running well as a puppy, but when an old dog it took some luck and a better animal to beat him. These dogs are, however, difficult to train, for as puppies they are very fast and terribly wild and headstrong. When once finished it is not easy to find their superiors. Mr. Johnson's Pitti Sing, purchased at Aldridge's in 1888, was of this strain, and she ran second in a stake in which each trial had to last four hours, and this competition took place in North Carolina. She ran three such trials, and only lost because she was not trained to retrieve, which all American and Canadian shooting dogs are expected to be.

At the National Trials in 1892 Colonel Cotes ran a puppy called Dash, which was the result of the first cross between a Gordon Setter of Lord Cawdor's strain and an English setter. It performed very well, indeed; so well, in fact, as to win the stake, and make one believe that a combination of the strains would lead to working animals that would probably have no superior. However the later or a continuation of the cross was not successful, and I believe Colonel Cotes did not persevere with it further. This dog had a fine nose, carried his head well, quartered his ground beautifully, and appeared to be persevering throughout, his natural qualities being good; and I take it that in the latter most important attributes " Stonehenge " considered the early Laveracks deficient. I do not think those that I have seen run from Mr. Llewellin's kennels of recent years are to be found fault with either as regards their pace or other capabilities. I fancy it was in 1889 that a nine months' old puppy of Mr. Llewellin's was entered at the National Trials, when he ran over a rough fallow, and by no means a level one either, in such a perfect, natural style, and at such a pace that I with others thought the stake at his mercy. However some trivial fault later on put him out of court.

Some years before this there was a much lauded setter called Ranger, whose pace and nose were such as to make him almost invincible. Unfortunately, I never saw him run, and have heard so many different opinions as to his merits that I can say very little upon the subject. He was an uncertain dog, but, this notwithstanding, he must be included with the dogs of his time—such as Count Wind'em, Phantom, Drake, Dash II., and Belle; with Countess and Nellie, who, at the Vaynol trials, in 1872, ran so well as a brace that they were given by the judges the full hundred points—as near the head of his race, and it has been said of him that when in the humour he was " as steady and dependable as a steam locomotive." During Ranger's career from 1873 to 1877 he won seven stakes and special prizes, and, if at times his work was not quite perfect, he, in the opinion of the judges, usually made up for some little delinquency by finding and standing birds in an extraordinary and brilliant manner. Ranger was a plain-looking—indeed, an ugly little dog, white with black and slight tan marks. He was bred by Mr. Macdona from his Judy by Paul Hackett's Rake—Calver's Countess; his sire being Quince II. by Jones' Quince I.—Lort's Dip.

An interesting trial would, no doubt, have been fought could he have been brought against Dr. Wood's lemon and white Fred W. who proved himself one of the best field trial dogs of more recent years. Unfortunately, Fred had not a long reign, flourishing, as our history would say, between 1891-92, both dates inclusive. Bred by Mr. T. Webber, of Falmouth, in August, 1886, Fred W. was by Prince W.—Moll W.; Prince by Sam IV.—Moll III.; Sam by young Rollick—Nell; but Fred W's. dam does not appear in the stud books. He was a lemon and white ticked dog, well made and symmetrical, but scarcely up to high-class show form in appearance, his head being more characteristic of the Irish rather than of the English setter. Fred W. made his mark as a Field Trial dog, and perhaps on all points had never many superiors; although, on his first appearance in 1890, he was put out of the aged competition at the National Trials because he failed to back, and Mr. Llewellin's Satin Bondhu won the stake. The latter, if not quite so fast as Fred W. had shown a better nose by finding birds the scent of which Dr. Wood's dog failed to hit, though the latter was well in front at the time. As is the case with almost all fast dogs, this failing to back was, at any rate in the early portion of his career, Fred W.'s chief defect. He won four stakes outright, the special cup on two occasions, once he was placed third only, when without injustice he should have been second, and on two other occasions he owed defeat to his unwillingness to back a point made by his opponent. Fred W., who had always been a delicate dog, died during the summer of 1892. He left a reputation as a Stud dog so far as field trials were concerned, and several of our chief performers of to-day have some of Fred W.'s blood in their veins. Prince Frederick and Fancy Free were perhaps the best of his actual progeny both running with great success in the spring of 1893.

Most of the best bench setters of modern times have come from the Ravensbarrow kennels of Mr. Cockerton, who has had them for some forty years, though he did not commence showing, excepting at a local gathering, until about 1881, since which time he has taken pretty much all before him, especially in the bitch classes at Birmingham. His best dogs have been Sir Simon, Madame Rachael, Cash in Hand, Belle of Furness, Monk of Furness, Ellen Terry, and Lady Bentinck, as with Lord Bentinck, now the property of Colonel Platt, and there are more whose names do not occur to me. Mr. John Shorthose, of Newcastle, has winning dogs of much the same strain; so have Mr. G. Cartmel, Kendal; Mr. G. E. Pridmore, Coleshill; Mr. T. Steadman, Merioneth-shire; Mr. G. Potter, Carlisle; Sir Humphrey de Trafford; Mr. Robertshaw, Lancashire; and others.

Mr. W. Hartley, Kendal, has had good dogs of this blood, Mr. W. H. B. Cockerton's Lune Belle, the writer's Richmond, and Sir H. de Trafford's Barton Tory being the best of his, and he who breeds such a brace and a half in a lifetime cannot be considered at all unlucky. At Birmingham, in 1892, the first two named, after winning in their respective classes, were placed first and third in competition for special prizes awarded to the best setters of all varieties afterwards.

Barton Tory, when little more than a puppy, made his *début* at Birmingham in 1896 where he did not gain all he ought to have done, for I considered him then the best English setter I ever saw, not excepting

Mr. Llewellin's cracks and such dogs as Richmond and Monk of Furness, both of which won all down the line whenever shown until 1896. Richmond was the champion at Birmingham for three years in succession, and in 1894 he won the special for the best setter of any variety in the show, and eventually found a new home in Melbourne, Australia.

A statement appeared in the *Kennel Gazette* not long ago, hinting that the English setter was not only degenerating, but rapidly disappearing. Such, however, is by no means the case, and, with the encouragement given by the various clubs and the trouble taken by breeders, this dog appears to be going rather strongly at the time I write. In the public field Mr. F. Lowe's Mabel of Kippen, a liver and white smart little bitch, has never had a superior, and, after doing remarkably well whenever she competed, she finished a brilliant service in 1896 by winning the chief stake at the International Trials at Bala, and later near Bordes, in France, added another £100 prize to the already long list which she had brought to her owner. Then the late Mr. Heywood-Lonsdale retained many good setters in his kennels; Ightfield Tom, a recent winner at work to wit; Sybarite Sam, too, must also be mentioned, and Mr. Llewellin's still strong team is alluded to elsewhere.

Sir Humphrey de Trafford, at Trafford Park, Manchester, has got together an extraordinarily fine team of English setters, workmen and bench winners. His Grouse of Kippen, a Welsh-bred dog, has done exceedingly well in both capacities; his Barton Charmer is as good as they can be made for work, whilst on the bench Mallwyd Flo, Mallwyd Bess, and Barton Tory formed a team good enough to beat all the other setters at Birmingham in 1896. Colonel Platt, at Llanfairfechan, is breeding some excellent setters, Madryn Earl, a field trial winner (and he has more good enough to take high honours anywhere), being perhaps the pick of his basket. Mr. Elias Bishop, Mr. F. Alexander, Mr. James Bishop, Mr. W. H. David (Neath), and Messrs. Bottomley (Bradford) may also be alluded to in addition to those already mentioned as owners of English setters quite equal to the average dog of previous years, and the entries at the Kennel Club show and at the National Exhibition in 1896 were quite as numerous, and all round of as good quality as one can expect to see in these days of hyper-criticism. It is pleasing also to be able to state that just now increasing attention is being paid to the working qualities and capabilities of the animals, and so long as we retain such dogs as those already named, and others perhaps equally good, or better, that have not appeared in public, there is little likelihood of the English setter lapsing into oblivion.

The best colours for these improved or modern Laveracks are blue or black and white flecked or ticked (Blue Beltons, as Mr. Laverack was the first to call them, taking this name from a village or hamlet in Northumberland), orange and white flecked, lemon and white ticked, black tan and white, and liver and white flecked. The orange, lemon, and liver or brown, are found in various shades, but the lighter hues are the most desirable.

Allusion has already been made to the setters bred by Mr. Purcell-Llewellin, and by many persons, both in this country and America, known as the " Llewellin " Setter. Whether the strain has by its characteristics merited a distinguishing title of its own is a question upon which opinions are divided, but, as to the excellence of the breed in work, and many of them in appearance, there cannot be two opinions In the field and on the moors they hold their own anywhere ; but of late years Mr. Llewellin's dogs have not been shown so much as they had been earlier on. Yet, when they do appear, they still come pretty forward in the prize list. I was much struck with the size and amount of bone a team of his possessed, which were in the ring at Birmingham in 1896, and this, notwithstanding their almost continuous inter-breeding. At the same time, in most other kennels, the tendency is to produce small and comparatively weedy animals.

The following interesting description of the Llewellin setter with which I have been favoured will, I believe, form a valuable contribution on a subject with which the admirers of the strain are not well acquainted :

" This is a strain of English setter, formed by its owner, Mr. R. Ll. Purcell-Llewellin, of Dorrington, near Shrewsbury. The late Mr. Laverack, in his book ' The Setter,' describes him as one ' who has endeavoured, and is still endeavouring, by sparing neither expense nor trouble, to bring to perfection the setter,' and has for over thirty years experimented largely in breeding and crossing strains of setters. In due course he succeeded in producing the remarkable family of setters which now bears his name.

" Mr. Llewellin many years ago kept black and tan setters; though he did not in those days exhibit. These dogs, however, although he spent much time and pains over their breeding, fell short of the ideal in his mind of the highest type of sportsman's dog, and, having moors in Scotland, and shootings in England and Wales, to test his ideas on, he, rightly or wrongly, was fully persuaded in his own mind that it was hopeless to spend more time over the black and tans; and, after full consideration, he finally discarded them. This conclusion was not come to without long trial and experiment of all the best strains of the day, having, besides the well known sorts, many of a kind not generally known, such as those of Mr. Hall, master of the Holderness, and, above all, those of his intimate friend 'Sixty-one' (the Rev. Hely Hutchinson), which were bred and used long before the days of dog shows for work in the Lews, where 'Sixty-one' for many years held some 70,000 acres of moors. Mr. Llewellin had his own reasons for discarding black and tans after experience of them for several years.

"He next tested the Irish setter, and in experimenting with this breed he followed on the same lines as in the case of their forerunners, the black and tans, *i.e.*, sparing no expense and trouble to get at the best possible specimens, and to try as many of the leading strains as possible. We find him therefore purchasing for £150 the famous 'Plunket' from Mr. Macdona, and dogs from the breed of the Knight of Kerry, from Colonel Whyte, of Sligo, from those of Cecil Moore, Colonel Hutchinson, Mr. Jephson, and several others. With these he bred, and some of the produce he exhibited, and his Kite,

Samson, Knowing, Carrie and Marvel, were excellent specimens of the Irish setter, winning him prizes on the show bench ; whilst Kite, Marvel, and Samson, were successful in field competition.

"Nevertheless, after long trial, Mr. Llewellin reluctantly confessed that, though superior to the black and tans, there were certain peculiarities in the Irish setter which he wished to see modified. Hereupon he commenced a long course of blending and crossing of these breeds with others. The result of one of these experiments was a handsome bitch, called Flame, a show winner, and for reasons which Mr. Llewellin deemed sufficient, he sold her. The blood of this bitch is still to be found in many of our leading bench winners at the present time.

"With all these crosses, however, Mr. Llewellin failed to satisfy his aspirations for a perfect working setter. Handsome many of them were, but he desired to develop certain peculiar field styles and methods of hunting in them, and which, as yet, neither the comparatively pure breeds alluded to, nor the crosses, had shown themselves possessed of.

"Mr. Laverack's breed was just about that time at its zenith, and, attracting Mr. Llewellin's attention, he hoped that at last he might obtain, in the so-called 'pure Laveracks,' what he had been seeking. He therefore, at a high price, secured the choicest Laverack blood, *i.e.*, that of Dash—Moll, and Dash—Lill. By this means Mr. Llewellin had succeeded so far in gaining all he desired, owning, as he now did, the Beautiful Countess, and her half sister Nellie, and later on, Mr. Garth's Daisy, three of the most famous Laveracks in the field that ever lived. He also owned Prince, brother to Nellie, a very handsome blue belton dog and a great show winner for his enterprising owner, who, moreover, owned Lill and Rock, the latter afterwards drafted by him and known as Lort's Jock. Mr. Llewellin bred several pure Laveracks, amongst which were the handsome bitches Phantom, Puzzle, Princess, all great show winners.

" Now, although Mr. Llewellin thus had the best possible opportunities and means of estimating the Laverack breed, he finally came to the conclusion that, however handsome at that time they were, and in the case of Countess, Nellie, and Daisy, good in some respects in the field, yet that, on the average, the pure Laveracks had too many unsatisfactory and inconvenient peculiarities of mind, habit, and instinct, to fit them for attaining his ideal. This discovery set Mr. Llewellin once again on the track of experiment, and, this time, with far more satisfaction to himself than anything he had previously experienced.

The result was the breed of dogs which bears his name, and which has scored its mark so deeply in setter history. Mr. Teasdale Buckel, the gentleman who handled so many of his winners at field trials in former years, materially assisted in showing this variety to the world.

"The particular strain which is known as the 'Llewellin' setter is, therefore, a blend of the pure Dash—Moll and Dash—Lill Laverack, with blood represented by Sir Vincent Corbet's Old Slut, and with that of the late Mr. Statter's Rhœbe, as shown chiefly in Dick, Dan, Dora, Daisy, Ruby, &c., but, whilst those for the most part were somewhat coarse, withal powerful workmanlike dogs, the Llewellin combination has retained the size, bone, and power, and added improvement in shape and make, so that the tendency towards coarseness, slackness of loin, and want of refinement, has been improved away, and the characteristic of the Llewellin is size with quality. That they possess quality and beauty of appearance their show bench achievements have proved, whilst at the same time their field trial record as a setter kennel has never been approached.

"In the days when the feeling for show bench honours was keener in Mr. Llewellin, his kennel had only to put in an appearance at a show to take nearly all the prizes. For years this was the case at the two great gatherings, Birmingham and London, the only places where they were exhibited.

"The sight presented by the setter benches in 1884, the first year that the Birmingham authorities offered special prizes for field trial winners, is well remembered by sportsmen. On that occasion Mr. Llewellin entered twelve field trial winners, viz., Count Wind'em, Dashing Bondhu, Dashing Duke, Sable Bondhu, Novel, Dashing Beauty, Dashing Ditto, Countess Bear, Countess Moll, Countess Rose, Nora, and Norna. Although there were some absentees, the team made a show of setters in itself, representing field as well as show champions—Count Wind'em, a field trial and also bench show champion, for whom Mr. Llewellin had been offered, and refused, £750 and £1200 ; Novel, equally a champion winner in the field and bench shows ; and that beautiful bitch Countess Bear, winner of the first field trial ' Derby,' besides other field trials, and several show prizes, both here and in America. Countess Rose was also a bench winner, and with Novel, winner of the Braces Stakes at one of the National Field Trial Meetings, on which occasion that well known judge, the late Sir Vincent Corbet, declared them the best brace he had ever seen. For these two bitches Mr. Llewellin was offered on the spot £1000. This same Birmingham team likewise included three winners of the field trial 'Derby,' Countess Bear, already alluded to; Sable Bondhu, and Dashing Ditto; also Norna, Nora, and Dashing Beauty, all gainers of first prizes at field trials; besides Dashing Bondhu, who up to quite recently had the record as a field trial winner, and it must be recollected that when he ran, meetings were not so numerous as they are now.

"The peculiarity of this kennel is that the same dogs unite in themselves, in a measure no others have done, first class show, as well as field trial quality. There are owners who have dogs with which they win on the bench but not in the field. Others, again, there are, which perform in the field but would take a low place at a show. The Llewellin dogs, on the contrary, have proved themselves capable bench show champions; yet the doings of the self-same dogs at field trials would alone have been sufficient to place them at the head of the list, even if they had possessed no other qualification.

"Mr. Llewellin has never, at any time, cared to keep so large a kennel as some other setter breeders, nor does he rear many during the year, a fact which should not be lost sight of when the large proportion of show and field trial prizes which have fallen to his setters is considered.

"The 'blue ribbon,' of field trials is held to be the 'Braces Stakes,' and, next in estimation is the field trial 'Derby,' the latter being a Kennel Club event, and the former that of the National Society. Mr. Llewellin's setters have won the 'Braces Stakes' twelve times, and the 'Derby' four times, whilst running second for those events on additional occasions. The 'Derby' was won three years in succession by his dogs Sable Bondhu, Dashing ditto, and Dashing Clinker. On the occasion when Sable won in 1882, three other puppies from the same kennel ran, and the four were placed equal, though the owner preferred that Sable Bondhu should have the honour, and so she was selected to run against the winning pointer puppy for the championship, which, as indicated above, she won. When Clinker won in 1883 something of the same happened, as he, with his kennel companion Duke Phœnix, had beaten all the other puppies, and Clinker was given the honour of running against the best pointer puppy, which he beat and so won the great prize.

"Mr. Llewellin did not compete at the Kennel Club trials from 1883 to 1893 but in 1894, he had several entries and up to 1896 quite held his own whenever his dogs were running. Daphne, Rosa Wind'em, Nelly Wind'em, Bruce Wind'em, Darkie

Wind'em, Jessie Wind'em and Daphne, being the best of his dogs of late years and not long ago Bruce Wind'em was sent over to the Imperial Kennels at St. Petersburg.

"It should be noted that several leading American sportsmen imported some of Mr. Llewellin's dogs several years ago, and that their workmanlike qualities and suitability to the peculiarities of American field sport brought them rapidly into favour, both in the States and Canada. The place they hold both at bench shows and field trials in that country is quite as prominent as it has been in the one of their origin. It is a question, however, whether the breed as it is now preserved in America is in all respects up to its original standard.

"It is interesting to state that Mr. Llewellin has never departed from the lines of blood with which he began to form his breed nearly twenty-five years ago. No outside cross of any sort or kind has been allowed to invade those lines. The various families are strictly preserved, and the strong family likeness, with the peculiar habits and methods of working, and their power to transmit those to others, justify, I consider, their title to rank as a distinct breed, which fact is perhaps more fully recognised in America than here."

From time to time there have cropped up

other so-called strains of English setters, but they have never possessed sufficiently distinguishing features to entitle them to a name or classification of their own. Personally, I have known more than one breed that better deserved a position of their own than some that strived to attain it. In Westmorland, fifteen or twenty years ago, the shooting men in the neighbourhood of Crosthwaite had black setters, not more than forty pounds in weight, with little coat and no lumber about them. They did not gallop at a very great pace, because the small allotments there were not suitable for fast dogs, but their noses were excellent; they required little training, and had stamina enough to hunt every alternate day during the season. No doubt, this was the remaining strain of the black setter Laverack alluded to in his book, as belonging to Harry "Rothwell." This I take to be a mistake for Rauthmell, whose family I knew very well. They lived not very far away from Crosthwaite, where Squire Rauthmell's hounds repeatedly went to hunt, and the two "country-sides" had much in common in the way of sport. I believe that in Wales there was a similar strain of setter to this, which has likewise been lost—perhaps by continual inter-breeding.

Another strain of setters I saw in the north many years ago were of a pale red colour, with a double nose. The owner said "they were the best in the world," but difficult to rear, and they seldom produced more than a brace or three puppies at a time. I fancy both these families have disappeared with the "statesmen" of the dales who shot over their own land, and could go over that of their neighbour were the latter not a sportsman himself. The surroundings of shooting have of late years changed in the north, and with this change such strains of setters as I have alluded to have gradually been allowed to die out.

There was another valued strain to be found in the kennels of the Marquis Breadalbane, and which I should not be surprised to find that Mr. Laverack had used freely. They were called "red marbles" or "blue marbles," the latter word possessing a similar meaning to that we attach to "mottle," "ticked," or "flecked." Of this strain were a brace or two that "Sixty-one" owned, on which he set great store, and called Balloch setters. They were long, low dogs, with great bone; they had nicely-shaped, but rather short, heads; their peculiarity lay in having a thick coat of, so to say, "fur," almost wool, at the roots of the ordinary jacket—an undercoat, in fact, like that a good collie should possess. No doubt the extra coat, not noticeable without examination, was provided by nature to withstand the cold climate in which they lived all the year round. In other respects both coat and feather were soft and silky. These dogs were excellent in the field, carrying their heads high, and working for the body scent in beautiful style. I believe, too, that Mr. Llewellin had one or two of these setters, and his opinion of them as working dogs was high.

Much has at times been written of the Llanidloes setter, which, as its name implies, has its habitat in Wales. At a show at Welshpool, in 1889, a class was provided for them, but no prizes were awarded. The chief exhibitor was Mr. J. J. W. Dashwood, of Huntington Court, Kingston, Hereford. It seems to me that this Welsh setter is no more than an ordinary English setter, with little distinguishing type, excepting a coarse, hard, curly coat, and a thick, though long, head, may be deemed to constitute a type, which I do not think is the case. It bears a reputation as a close, slow, and methodical worker, and better able to perform the duties of an all-round dog in a rough country than the much more highly bred animal, which is, however, fast supplanting the older-fashioned and more spaniel-like article. From what I have heard by men who have used the Llanidloes setter, it appears to be hardy, is not spoiled by being allowed to hunt covert for cock and pheasant, and is thoroughly suitable for a "one dog man."

The Anglesea setter, the Newcastle setter, the Featherstone setter, and others that could be mentioned are but local strains of the general variety as it is diffused throughout the country. In no case have they been kept sufficiently pure to justify anyone placing them as varieties of their own. The Earl of Tankerville has had good setters, and so has Lord Waterpark; likewise, Mr. Jones of Oscot, the late Mr. F. R. Bevan, the late Mr. W. Lort, Mr. Bayley, Colonel Cotes, Mr. R. Lloyd Price, Mr. T. Cunnington, and Mr. Paul Hackett, but they laid no claim to any particular strain of their own.

The Russian setter has often been alluded to by previous writers. "Stonehenge" gives us a picture of one, but such a dog has either died out altogether or been returned to the country that gave him birth. As a fact I do not believe the Russians ever had a setter of their own. For years Mr. Purcell Llewellin offered a prize for him at the Birmingham show, but in no instance was there an entry forthcoming. Possibly, in promising such a thing the Welsh squire was poking fun at the breed, and, in a way of his own, endeavouring to prove to the public what he thought himself, that such a thing as a "Russian setter" had only existence in fancy.

Our English Setter Club was formulated in 1890; following, a description of the breed was drawn up and adopted, and I fancy its foundation was taken from Mr. Laverack's description in his book. However, I with others do not consider the club standard by any means what it ought to be, so in preference to theirs I give one of my own, which in the main is similar to " Stonehenge's " which is so generally adopted.

1. The *skull* (value 5) has a character peculiar to itself. It possesses considerable prominence of the occipital bone ; is moderately narrow between the ears ; and there is a decided brow over the eyes. A sensible forehead with width enough for brains.

2. The *nose* (value 5) should be long and wide, without any fullness under the eyes. There should be in the average dog setter at least four inches from the inner corner of the eye to the end of the nose. Between the point and the root of the nose there should be a slight depression—at all events there should be no fullness—and the eyebrows should rise sharply from it. The nostrils must be wide apart and large in the openings, and the end should be moist and cool, though many a dog with good scenting powers has had a dry nose. In dark coloured specimens the nose should be black, but in

the orange and whites, or lemon and whites, a coloured nose is desirable, though it must not be spotted. The jaws should be exactly equal in length, "pig jaw," as the receding lower one is called, being greatly against its possessor, nor should he be undershot.

3. *Ears, lips,* and *eyes* (value 10).—With regard to ears, they should be small, shorter than a pointer's. The "leather" should be thin and soft, carried closely to the cheeks, almost folding from their roots, so as not to show the inside, without the slightest tendency to prick; the ear should be partly clothed with silky hair, but there must not be too much of it. The lips also are not so full and pendulous as those of the pointer, but at their angles there should be a slight fullness, not reaching quite to the extent of hanging. The eyes must be full of animation, and of medium size, the best colour being dark brown, and they should be set with their angles straight across. The head and expression of the English setter are pleasing.

4. The *neck,* (value 5) has not the full rounded muscularity of the pointer, being considerably thinner, but still slightly arched. It must not be "throaty," though the skin is loose.

5. The *shoulders* and *chest* (value 15) should display great liberty in all directions, with sloping

deep shoulder blades, and elbows well let down. The chest should be deep rather than wide. The ribs well sprung behind the shoulder, and great depth of the back ribs should be especially demanded.

6. *Back, quarters,* and *stifles* (value 15).—An arched loin is desirable, but not to the extent of being " roached " or " wheel-backed," a defect which generally tends to a slow up-and-down gallop. Stifles well bent, and set wide apart, to allow the hind legs to be brought forward with liberty in the gallop.

7. *Legs, elbows,* and *hocks* (value 12).—The elbows and toes, which generally go together, should be set straight; and if not, the " pigeon-toe " or inturned leg is less objectionable than the out-turn, in which the elbow is confined by its close attachment to the ribs. The arm should be muscular, and the bone fully developed, with strong and broad knees, short, well turned pasterns, of which the size in point of bone should be as great as possible (a very important point), and their slope not exceeding a very slight deviation from the straight line. The hind legs should be muscular, with plenty of bone, clean strong hocks, and hairy feet.

8. The *feet* (value 8).—A difference of opinion exists as to the comparative merit of the cat and hare foot for standing work. Masters of foxhounds

invariably select that of the cat, and, as they have better opportunities than any other class for instituting the necessary comparison, their selection may be accepted as final. But, as setters are specially required to stand wet and heather, it is imperatively necessary that there should be a good growth of hair between the toes, and on this account a longer but thick foot, well clothed with hair on and between the toes is preferred. This hair on and between the toes acts as a protection on rough stony ground, and it is said that amongst the flints of some countries a setter can on this account work for a day where a pointer would be placed *hors de combat* in half an hour.

9. The *flag* (value 5) is in appearance characteristic of the breed, although it sometimes happens that one or two puppies in a well-bred litter exhibit a curl or other malformation, usually considered to be indicative of a stain. The setter's flag should have a gentle sweep downwards; and the nearest resemblance to any familiar form is to the scythe with its curve reversed. The feather must be composed of straight silky hairs; close to the root the less hair the better, and again towards the point, of which the bone should be fine, and the feather tapering with it.

10. *Symmetry and quality* (value 10). — In

character the setter should display a great amount of " quality," which means a combination of symmetry, as understood by the artist, with the peculiar attributes of the breed under examination, as interpreted by the sportsman. Thus, a setter possessed of such a frame and outline, as to charm the former would be considered by the sportsman defective in " quality " if he possessed a curly or harsh coat, or if he had a heavy head, with pendant bloodhoundlike jowl and throaty neck. The general outline is elegant, and very taking to the eye.

11. The *texture and feather* of coat (value 5) are much regarded, a soft silky hair without curl being a *sine qua non*. The feather should be considerable, and should fringe the hind as well as the fore legs.

12. The *colour of coat* (value 5) is not much insisted on, a great variety being admitted. These are as follows: Black and white ticked, with large splashes, and more or less marked with black, known as " blue belton;" orange and white, ticked and marked as in the blacks or blues; liver and white, ticked in a similar manner; black and white with tan markings; orange or lemon and white ticked; black and white; liver and white. Pure white, black, liver, and red or yellow are sometimes seen, but are not desirable.

Weight, dogs from 48lb. to 60lb.; bitches from 40lb. to 50lb.

	Value.		Value.
Skull	5	Legs, elbows, and hocks	12
Nose	5	Feet	8
Ears, lips, and eyes	10	Flag	5
Neck	5	Symmetry and quality	10
Shoulders and chest	15	Coat	5
Back, quarters, and stifles	15	Colour	5
	—		—
	55		45

Grand Total 100.

J. T. Kent's, 2009 Walnut Street, Philadelphia, Pa.
KENT RODERIGO.

THE SETTER (ENGLISH).

ORIGIN.—Best authorities claim it to be descended from the old Spanish setting-spaniel.

USES.—Hunting all kinds of game-birds.

* SCALE OF POINTS, ETC.

	Value.			Value.
Skull	5	Feet	. 8
Nose	5	Flag	. 5
Ears, lips, and eyes .	. 10	Symmetry and quality .	. 10
Neck	5	Coat	. 5
Shoulders and chest .	. 15	Color	. 5
Back, quarters, and stifles	. 15		
Legs, elbows, and hocks	. 12	Total . .	. 100

HEAD.—Considerable prominence of occipital bone, moderately narrow between ears, with decided brow over eyes. Nose long, wide, without fullness under eye; nostrils large and wide apart. Dark specimens should have black nose; for orange and whites, or lemon and whites, a colored nose is desirable. Jaws level, and of equal length. Ears small, shorter than a pointer's, and carried close to cheeks, partly clothed with silky hair; leather thin and soft.

Lips not full nor pendulous. Eyes medium size, animated, best colors being brown.

NECK.—Not throaty; skin rather loose; slightly arched.

SHOULDERS AND CHEST.—Shoulders sloping; elbows well let down; chest deep; ribs well sprung, with great depth of back ribs.

BACK.—Arched over loins, but not wheel-back; stifles well bent, set wide apart.

LEGS, ELBOWS, AND TOES.—Legs straight; arms muscular; knees broad and strong; pasterns short; hind legs muscular, plenty of bone; hocks clean and strong.

FEET.—Either cat- or harefoot; but either must be well clothed with hair and between toes.

FLAG.—Sweeps gently downward; feather plenty, straight and silky.

COAT.—Soft, silky, without curl.

COLOR.—Black and white, ticked with large splashes and more or less marked with black; orange and white, liver and white, ticked as above; black and white, ticked with tan markings; orange or lemon and white; black and white; liver and white.

· ENGLISH · SETTERS ·

Gentlemen's Shooting Dogs
a Specialty. ✺✺✺✺✺✺✺✺✺✺
Broken, Unbroken Dogs, and
Puppies, also Brood Bitches.

Any one about to purchase a gentleman's shooting
dog is requested to visit BELLEPLAIN and shoot over
these dogs until suited.

KENT RODERIGO at Stud.   A. K. C. 42253.   Vol. 13.

BELLEPLAIN KENNELS,

Belleplain, N. J.

DR. J. T. KENT,   JOSEPH MASON,
Proprietor.   Superintendent.

Mr. H. K. Bloodgood's (Mepal Kennels, New Marlboro, Mass.)
"QUEEN B"

THE ENGLISH SETTER

Origin.—The best authorities claim it to be descended from the old Spanish setting-spaniel.

Uses.—Hunting all kinds of game-birds.

*STANDARD.

Skull.—Has a character peculiar to itself. It possesses considerable prominence of the occipital bone; is moderately narrow between the ears; and there is a decided brow over the eyes. A sensible forehead with width enough for brains.

Nose.—Long and wide, without any fullness under the eyes. There should be in the average dog setter at least four inches from the inner corner of the eye to the end of the nose. Between the point and the root of the nose there should be a slight depression—at all events there should be no fullness—and the eyebrows should rise sharply from it. The nostrils must be wide apart and large in the openings, and the end should be moist and cool, though many a dog with good scenting powers has had a dry nose. In dark colored specimens the nose should be black, but in the orange and whites, or lemon and whites, a colored nose is desirable, though it must not be spotted. The jaws should be exactly equal in length, "pig jaw" as the receding lower one is called, being greatly against its possessor, nor should he be under-shot.

83

Ears, Lips and Eyes.—With regard to ears, they should be small, and shorter than a pointer's. The leathers should be thin and soft, carried closely to the cheeks, almost folding from their roots, so as not to show the inside, without the slightest tendency to prick; the ear should be partly clothed with silky hair, but there must not be too much of it. Lips also are not so full and pendulous as those of the pointer, but at their angles there should be a slight fullness, not reaching quite to the extent of the hanging. Eyes must be full of animation, and of medium size, the best color being dark brown, and set with their angles straight across. The head and expression of the English setter are pleasing.

Neck.—Has not the full rounded muscularity of the pointer, being considerably thinner, but still slightly arched. It must not be "throaty," though the skin is loose.

Shoulders and Chest.—Should display great liberty in all directions with sloping deep shoulder blades, and elbows well let down. Chest should be deep rather than wide. Ribs well sprung behind the shoulder, and great depth of the back ribs should be especially demanded.

Legs, Elbows and Hocks.—Elbows and toes, which generally go together, should be set straight; and if not, the "pigeon toe" or inturned leg is less objectionable than the out-turn, in which the elbow is confined by its close attachment to the ribs. The arm should be muscular, and the bone fully developed, with strong and broad knees, short, well-turned pasterns, of which the size in point of bone should be as great as possible, (a very important point) and their slope not exceeding a very slight deviation from the straight line. Hind legs muscular, with plenty of bone, clean, strong hocks and hairy feet.

Back, Quarters and Stifles.—An arched loin is desirable, but not to the extent of being "roached" or "wheel-backed," a defect which generally tends to a slow up-and-down gallop. Stifles well bent, and set wide apart, to allow the hind legs to be brought forward with liberty in the gallop.

Feet.—A difference of opinion exists as to the comparative merit of the cat and hare foot for standing work. Masters of foxhounds invariably select that of the cat, and, as they have better opportunities than any other class for instituting the necessary comparison, their selection may be accepted as final. But, as setters are especially required to stand wet and heather, it is imperatively necessary that there should be a good growth of hair between the toes, and on this account a longer but thick foot well clothed with hair on and between the toes is preferred. This hair on and between the toes acts as a protection on rough, stony ground, and it is said that amongst the flints of some countries a setter can on this account work a day where a pointer would be placed *hors de combat* in half an hour.

Flag.—Is in appearance characteristic of the breed, although it sometimes happens that one or two puppies in a well-bred litter exhibit a curl or other malformation, usually considered to be indicative of a stain. The setter's flag should have a gentle sweep downwards, and the nearest resemblance to any familiar form is to the scythe with its curve reversed. The feather must be composed of straight silky hairs; close to the root, the less hair the better, and again towards the point, of which the bone should be fine, and the feather tapering with it.

Mr. Jos. B. Vandergrift's (Vancroft Kennels, late Lemington Kennels, Pittsburgh, Pa.)
"BARTON TORY"

Symmetry and Quality.—In character the setter should display a great amount of "quality" which means a combination of symmetry, as understood by the artist, with the peculiar attributes of the breed under examination, as interpreted by the sportsman. Thus, a setter possessed of such a frame and outline as to charm the former would be considered by the sportsman defective in "quality" if he possessed a curly or harsh coat, or if he had a heavy head, with pendant bloodhound-like jowl and throaty neck. The general outline is elegant, and very taking to the eye.

Texture and Feather of Coat.—These are much regarded, a soft silky hair without curl being a *sine qua non*. The feather should be considerable and should fringe the hind as well as the fore-legs.

Color of Coat.—Is not much insisted on, a great variety being admitted. These are as follows: Black and white ticked with large splashes, and more or less marked with black, known as "blue belton"; orange and white, ticked and marked as in the blacks or blues; liver and white, ticked in a similar manner; black and white with tan markings; orange or lemon and white ticked; black and white; liver and white. Pure white, black, liver, and red or yellow are sometimes seen, but are not desirable.

Weight.—Dogs from 48 to 60 lbs.; bitches from 40 to 50 lbs.

*SCALE OF POINTS.

Skull	5	Legs, elbows and hocks	12
Nose	5	Feet	8
Ears, lips and eyes	10	Flag	5
Neck	5	Symmetry and quality	10
Shoulders and chest	15	Coat	5
Back, quarters and stifles	15	Color	5

Total.. 100

85

The unfortunate state of affairs that exists at present in the ranks of the English setter fanciers makes it necessary for the foreign standard to be quoted here, and if it is faithfully lived up to the dog will in years be greatly improved and some sort of type be apparent at our shows. At present, and in fact for some years past, the English setter has been rapidly degenerating as a show dog, anything apparently that could win in a field trial being considered the proper dog to win on the bench and to breed to as well. The result is that we have as many different types winning today as Joseph of old had colors in his coat. It resolves itself into the indisputable fact that scarcely a single exhibitor of English setters can tell you at the opening of a show which dog will or should win. He simply don't know. As long as

Mr. John Brett's (Fisher's Island, N. Y.)
" CACTUS "

we have judges who can only see good in the style of dog that last won in the field trials, *and which changes at every field trial*, we may never hope to bring order out of the chaos that now exists and has existed for years. At last our fanciers realize "where they are at" and are scurrying to get straightened out. The endeavor is commendable but so very late. A decade or so ago, we had some sort of type to breed to for the show bench, but if anyone can tell the public what the type of the winning English setter of today is, he should be crowned "The King of the Solons" and half of dogdom would contribute generously towards the purchase of a suitable " head-piece." There is but one way out of it for the fancier who has the regeneration of the dog at heart and that is to begin all over and try to breed to the standard and not to the dog whose only recommendation is that he won at a certain field trial. Such fanciers as Messrs. Laverack and Llewellin would certainly feel that all their efforts to improve the breed had gone for naught were they to visit some of our shows today and witness the giving-out of the ribbons. (The word "giving-out" instead of "awarding the prizes" is here used advisedly.)

The standard rightly says that the head of the setter is peculiar to itself, and the further it is away from that of the spaniel the better. Fullness before the eyes is a most objectionable feature, as is a short muzzle, while in the same category we can well place the snipy or pig-jaw formations which too many of our setters possess. There should be good depth from the bridge of the nose to the lower part of the lip, the contour being very clear cut. Ears that are large, of heavy leather or set high on the head or away from it come under the head of "faults." Light eyes are almost universally condemned, the dark ones being the most acceptable. The setter is used for hunting birds and his neck therefore should be of good length so as to give him freedom of action. It is not so round as the pointer's and where that conformation exists it counts against the dog. Heavy shoulders, or those that are close together, are detrimental to the dog's free and easy action and should carry a penalty with them. They are wholly out of place in this breed. A shallow chest, or flat ribs, legs that are not straight, weak pasterns, lightness of bone, or absence of strength of loins are faults that cannot be overlooked in this dog. The hind-quarters, if light, or stifles, if straight, are two defects that militate greatly against a dog winning the highest prizes under good judges. The question of the proper sort of feet seems to have been settled in favor of the cat-foot well covered with hair, though there are some good judges who have a leaning for the hare-foot. The flag is certainly a characteristic feature of the setter, and nothing detracts more from his beauty than a failing in this point. One that is curly or is carried over the back or is short of feather is decidedly faulty. The coat to be true to the breed will be declared faulty if it is not straight and wholly free from curl, and the straighter it is the better. In the matter of colors, those that exist should be clear in themselves and be free from all appearance of smuttiness, one color standing out bold from the other. There have been some very good dogs that would have become famous winners had their color been correct.

The Westminster Kennel Club Show and other shows, in the year of grace 1901, have proved to a large number of lovers of the setter, whether it be of the English, Gordon or Irish branch of the family, that a diversity of opinion *really* does exist as to how the various breeds should be judged. The placing of Barton Tory in the position where his winning card showed him to be, produced a desired effect as well as verifying the old adage that there is no evil but has some good. This, however, is but little satisfaction to the owner of such a dog, except it be that it was a large factor in the calling together of "men who were the stand-bys of the English setter in the past" as well as "adopting a proper standard." It seems to all fanciers of this beautiful breed of dogs that the qualification of judges must rest, not in their popularity as "good fellows" but as keen observers and possessed of ability to balance the good with the bad qualities and arrive at a decision that will place each dog where he belongs.

THE ENGLISH SETTER

THE origin of the Setter is involved in hopeless mystery, and it would not be particularly interesting or of any great importance to endeavour to penetrate it by giving the various and irreconcilable opinions of many writers, both ancient and modern, who have given us their views on the subject. Suffice it to say that the general opinion that the Setter was the improved and selected offspring of the Springer Spaniel does not seem as probable as its converse.

There is no doubt but that the Setter was first used for hawking, and it seems far more probable that a pointing dog, rather than a flushing one, should have been acceptable for this purpose. Besides, the word Spaniel, or Spaynel, indicates Spain, as in an old book, said to be written by a son of Edward III. in 1402, it is stated : " The nature of him comes from Spain."

What appears most probable is that the Setter is the oldest of British dogs, that it was probably introduced by the Romans, and that, when in later times the Spaniel and Pointer were imported from Spain, crosses between these and the original English dog produced respectively the more modern Setter and the many different strains of Spaniels now so well known among us.

Between the old Springer and the modern Setter there is a strong family likeness, as may be seen by many plates of this dog published in old books. Setters and Pointers too were of course broken to the net long before guns were invented. Wood says : " The first person who broke a setting dog to the net was Dudley, Duke of Northumberland, in 1535 "; and as late as 1818 we hear of pointing dogs being used for this purpose, and to the writer's certain knowledge they have been employed by poachers very much later than that. For this purpose the Setter appears to have been preferred to the Pointer on account of his natural crouching attitude.

Perhaps there are very few sportsmen or dog lovers of the present day who would not agree with the opinion that the Setter is the most beautiful in appearance, as well as the most affectionate in disposition, of any sporting dog. Whether the beauty of the breed, as well as its sterling sporting qualities, has been improved in the last hundred years is an exceedingly doubtful matter. The writer inclines to a medium opinion—viz. that a hundred years ago there were a great many *more* really handsome dogs than there are now, and also a great many *more* really useful and dependable for shooting purposes, but that there are *a select few* to be found at the present day vastly superior certainly in beauty, possibly in working qualities, to their ancestors. His own recollection of the ancient Setter, which goes back to the year 1853, is that he distinctly remembers at that time three, if not four, distinctly different-looking dogs.

There were a great number of Setters in those days, mostly lemon-and-whites, in the South and West of England—great upstanding dogs with finé shoulders and hindquarters and exuberant feather. These may be taken as the pure breed. Again, there was another sort shorter in the leg, with heads broader and more massive, and coats inclined to be curly; these had no doubt been crossed with the Irish Water Spaniel. There was a third sort, of which the writer has seen but very few specimens, a short, stout dog with a short, broad nose, and as slow as a man ; this may be taken as a recent cross with the Spaniel.

The fourth sort was a small, fine-limbed, beautifully feathered, straight-coated dog, with a finely cut head, generally black-and-white. Mr. Hiles, the agent for Lady Bowden, in Herefordshire, had a strain of these. The writer bought one himself from him early in the fifties, and he was one of the best in the field he ever saw and as handsome as a picture.

Now, it is a common idea that there are a great many more Setters, and Pointers too, in these days than there were fifty years ago. The writer does not believe a word of it.

There are, we know, in the present day very large kennels of both breeds, chiefly kept for show and field-trial purposes ; but these are, after all, few and far between, while now, alas! even on the Scotch moors dogs are rarely used, and for partridge shooting we may almost say never. In the old days every man who shot had one or two dogs—no one ever shot without them—and some had fairly large kennels. Not only that fast-declining race the old English gentleman had his Setters or Pointers or both, but every sporting farmer likewise.

The writer has a vivid remembrance of a Setter belonging to a man of this then most worthy class, and with whom as a boy he had many a good day's sport. The dog was a huge black-and-white, nearly as big as a Newfoundland, with a massive Pointer head and a curly coat. He was very slow but exceedingly sure, and if you gave him plenty of time, he would range every inch of a field and find everything in it. His master was a fine fellow of 6ft. 3in., big in proportion, and immensely powerful, he was celebrated far and wide in the country for his pugilistic proclivities, and was, moreover, a really wonderful shot.

One day, while out with this man and dog, the writer hit a bird hard which went on over a small hanging wood and then towered. On arriving as promptly as possible at the spot, we found it was a potato garden, in which the occupier was apparently hard at work.

" Did you see that bird fall ? " said Mr. C——.

" No, sir ; no bird fell here."

" Ah ! " was the reply, with a knowing wink at me. " Here, then, we'll look for it." And beckoning his dog to the end of the little field to give him the wind, he gave him a cast straight across the potato digger.

The old dog threw his head up into the wind, walked a few yards, and then came to a dead point ten yards from the man. Mr. C—— walked up calmly, took his coat off, folded it up, and laid it on the ground.

" Now, then," he said, "give me that bird out of your pocket, or I'll give you the —— hiding you ever had in your life."

The man began, " I told ee——," and then, looking up and observing an ominous turning up of the shirt-sleeves, he took the bird out of his pocket and handed it over without a word.

" Whatever made you think of that ? " the writer said afterwards.

" Why, because last week old Don did the same thing, only that time it was at my coat, with a brace of birds in it, that I had put down on the ground while I walked a bit of standing wheat in the hot sun."

Now, if we think of the very large number of these sportsmen, both gentlemen and farmers, who all had dogs, we cannot help coming to the certain conclusion that Pointers and Setters were far more numerous in those days than in these ; and besides this, there can be no doubt whatever that their field qualities were, as a rule, vastly superior. Men in those days did not keep dogs for show or for swagger, neither did they keep them for the purpose of running them once or twice a year against Dick, Tom, and Harry ; they were not therefore, forsooth, afraid of spoiling them by shooting to them, as men are now. If they kept a dog, it *had* to be a good one to shoot to, or else it would very soon itself be shot.

In the South and West of England no strains, in the writer's opinion, were kept distinct ; if a man had a bitch good in the field, he would put her to an equally good dog belonging to some friend or neighbour, utterly regardless of make or shape : excellence in the field was the one thing needful. Dozens of names of men who had kennels like this before the days of dog shows could be mentioned. The late Mr. Calmady, a well-known sportsman and M.F.H., of Devon and Cornwall celebrity, had some beautiful lemon-and-whites. Mr. Webber, a Falmouth tradesman and a good old-fashioned sportsman, had a breed that he set great store by, though the specimens thereof were the most uneven that one can imagine in general form and also in working qualities. The writer remembers seeing from one litter that this gentleman bred a tall, long-headed, light, and airy brother, a beautiful goer and very good in the field, and a thick, cobby, bull-headed sister, as heavy as a cart-horse and practically useless.

The sporting county of Salop possessed one of the best and most famous old strains of Setter, that of the well-known baronet Sir Vincent Corbet, the portraits of many of which still adorn the walls of the hall at Acton Reynald. These dogs were lemon-and-white; and one of them, Slut, became by Sir F. Grahame's Duke the dam of another Duke, far famed as the ancestor of the best modern strains of Setter. This strain of Sir V. Corbet's seems also to have been in the possession of a Shrewsbury tradesman named Hall, and was crossed in later days with the Marquis of Anglesea's breed the Beaudesert black-white-and-tan, as well as with the Grahame as aforesaid.

The Border counties of Cumberland and Westmorland and the adjacent parts of Scotland boast themselves as having been the home *par excellence* of the Setter.

The Duke of Gordon's kennel, well known to fame, consisting for the most part of the colour black-white-and-tan, was no doubt the progenitor of a great part of the fashionable blood of both ancient and modern days, and the Lords Lovat, Seafield, Cawdor, and Southesk had notable strains. The Marquis of Breadalbane also had a strain known locally as "blue marbles" and "red marbles." No doubt all these breeds were at one time kept very jealously to themselves; indeed, as late as 1872 Lord Lovat's was preserved intact—at all events, was supposed to be; but a few years later the specimens had become smaller in size and were evidently deteriorating.

Most probably these strains were sooner or later mixed together, and many an offshoot must have come into the possession of local sportsmen. There was one curious peculiarity observed in many of these Scotch dogs—under the ordinary coat there was an underlayer of a sort of soft wool. This most probably originated from their having been kept for generations in exposed kennels in the cold north-country winters.

When paying a visit in the sixties to the kennels of the Rev. T. Pearce ("Idstone") at Morden, in Dorset, the writer recollects seeing there some very handsome Setters, black-white-and-tan, orange-and-white, lemon-and-white; these, it appears, Mr. Pearce was accustomed to buy through agents from Scotland at the close of the grouse season at very low prices, he would then put his "imprimatur" on them, and sell them again at high figures. These dogs

91

were far superior in appearance to most of the Setters of the present day, and were no doubt blends of these old strains. The writer saw some of them on partridges : they had good noses and style, but were not well broken.

Again, there seems to have been a distinct strain of Setter in Wales, though personally the writer has only seen two specimens, and they were short, cobby things like Spaniels, with long, curly ears and wavy coats.

And now we come to a very important epoch in dog history, the period of shows and then of field trials. The first Birmingham show was held in November, 1859. The entries were very few and the animals very imperfect. For the first few years the prize honours were chiefly gained by the Black-and-tans, or so-called Gordon Setters, and then there suddenly appeared on the scene a man called Laverack with some specimens of a kennel that he guaranteed had been bred from two ancestors for forty years, and these carried all before them.

Mr. Laverack and his Setters have had such a startling effect on the Setter world that they are worthy of some considerable comment. The history of Laverack himself is sufficiently interesting.

A native of some Westmorland village, he appears in his youth to have been a shoemaker's apprentice. Early in life, however, he came into possession of a legacy bequeathed to him by some distant relative. On this he appears to have been able to gratify the exceeding love for sport which was doubtless in his blood from some remote ancestor. In those days, which would be about 1825, there was any amount of grouse-shooting to be got for nothing by any one who was not afraid of roughing it, and Laverack appears to have led a nomadic life devoted to Setters and shooting for at least forty years. He was a good sportsman, and undoubtedly a most marvellous judge of dogs, and for that reason a most successful breeder of beauty and of some excellence.

It always seemed a great pity that he "gave himself away" to the public by publishing his miraculous in-and-in pedigrees, which can be seen in the Kennel Club Stud Book. He probably believed them to some extent himself, but whether he ever succeeded in inducing others to do so, with the exception perhaps of a very few, is far more dubious. To any man of common sense, not to speak of any practical experience, they are simply an impossibility. One thing is, however, certain, that his talent for selection enabled him to breed very closely, and so to preserve and increase the beauty of his type, and that his inherent canniness, as well as his perfect judgment, enabled him to select occasional fresh strains of blood, which improved instead of destroying the excellence of the progeny.

Sometimes also he, in the soothing atmosphere of a winter

evening's fire combined with the seductive effects of some good old port, disclosed a few faint shadows of his dark secrets. One of them is here related.

Once on a time there was a tract of country on the Borders called "the Debatable Land," nominally belonging to the Earls of Carlisle. Now, this country swarmed with gipsies, and that strange people had from time immemorial claimed the right to shoot over this tract at their own sweet will, so on August 12th in each year they were accustomed to form a band of thirty or more, and with a large army of Setters, and probably Pointers as well, make a regular raid on the said moors, and it is not surprising that the keepers gave them a wide berth.

Well, on one Twelfth, Laverack accompanied this mob, and he had with him one of his best dogs. Among all the Setters which were ranging far and wide, Laverack's keen eyes noted one animal, liver-and-white, which was *facile princeps*, and beat the whole lot in both nose and pace, though by no means a good-looking one. "Well, sir," the old man said, "I hunted up those gipsies. I found that dog, I bought him, and I bred from him!"

There is some reason to suspect that in much later times a judicious cross was effected with the Pointer; but there seems to be very little doubt at all that the Irish Setter also was called in to refresh the blood. The writer feels sure that the old man, in his later days, having sold all his best dogs at temptingly high prices, was *obliged*, in order to save his strain from utter extinction, to resort to some outside agency to preserve it, and there are some good judges who fancy that they can even now trace some of these crosses in the world-wide progeny that has resulted from the, in many cases, injudicious and indiscriminate use of the Laverack Setter with the old English strains.

Now, it is commonly said among Setter men that Laverack was a great benefactor to the Setter and the Setter lover. The writer's opinion is that this idea admits of very grave doubt. One thing seems certain—viz. that the Laverack and its crosses caused a great number of men to give up shooting over dogs altogether, and that for one simple reason only—viz. that they could not break either the original or its offspring. The ancient Laverack excelled in beauty, it also had surpassing good field qualities, a very high head, a wonderful nose, great pace, endurance, pluck, and a marvellous "sporting instinct." By this last is meant such a love for game-finding that it would go on for ever, even though never a bird was shot to it; but to all these qualities it added an almost invincible headstrongness and obstinacy, and this rendered it an impossible object of training to nine men out of ten, of that day at all events. So things happened thus: every one sought to cross his breed with a Laverack, of some sort or another, and

93

everybody did it; and so a headstrong breed arose which no one could manage, and therefore men went out shooting without their dogs. The writer recollects Laverack himself being once asked on the moors with respect to a dog of his, which was endued with perpetual motion, entire self-hunting, and utter regardlessness of whistle, "However do you get that dog home at night?" "Why, sir, I just wait till he points, and then I put a collar and chain on him and lead him home."

The writer firmly believes that if Laverack had never existed we should now have a more even and a far more useful Setter, and that many more would be used for shooting. The writer, indeed, had several friends, shooting comrades in those now ancient days, who discarded dogs simply because they could not manage them, and when they came to shoot with him and saw a brace of tremendous rangers put down, who would gallop like lightning, fall down motionless on point in their wild career, and take a fifty-acre field in one beat, they could not understand it; they could not believe that game was not left behind in those wide quarterings, and although the dogs might never make a mistake, they got so nervous they could not shoot, as they always thought the dogs were going to do some outrageous thing.

Mr. Laverack never called his dogs by his own name—that was the doing of the British public; indeed, he never claimed to have *invented* his strain, only to have *continued* it. Here are his own words, copied from a letter written by himself: "The breed of Setters that I have found most useful and valuable, combining the essential qualities of a setting dog—viz. innate point, speed, nose, method of range or carriage, with powers of endurance—has been known in the northern counties of Cumberland, Northumberland, and the southern counties of Scotland as the old original black or silver grey, and in Scotland as the old blue Beltons. How they originated I can't say; but I can state with confidence that I can trace back this breed for a period of seventy-five years or more, having had them in my own possession forty years, and the late Rev. A. Harrison, of Carlisle, from whom I originally obtained them, had them thirty-five years previously."

The pure Laverack Setter is now as nearly as possible extinct. Mr. Pilkington, of Sandside, Caithness, had, a few years since, and probably still has, a kennel of beautiful Setters, mostly blue Beltons, and these are as good on the moors as they are handsome in the kennel. Some of these may be pure Laveracks; at all events, they are very closely allied to the strain. Mr. Hartley also, a gentleman residing in Leicestershire, has some fine specimens of the " Pride of the Border" family of Laveracks, which he has kept intact. Of course there may be some others.

And now we come to the most celebrated strain of the modern

Setter—indeed, we may safely call it the only English Setter now existing that deserves the name of a distinct strain. This was originally evolved, and has been continued up to the present time, by the judgment and devotion of its founder, Mr. Richard Purcell Llewellin. Mr. Llewellin, the descendant of a noted old Welsh sportsman of that name, commenced Setter breeding very soon after the first inauguration of field trials, nearly forty years ago. He began with black-and-tans and with some of the old-fashioned English Setters. He entered these at trials and was badly beaten. He then purchased some of the finest and best Irish Setters that could be procured, and with them and their progeny he won extensively at dog shows and sometimes at trials. Not yet satisfied, he tried crossing the Irish with the Laverack, and obtained thereby some exceedingly handsome specimens, which at shows were well-nigh invincible. Among these he bred a bitch called Flame, a perfectly formed red-and-white of wonderful quality. This bitch, it is worthy of note, after being sold by him, became the ancestress of the fashionable show winners of past and present days, and perhaps there are very few of these winners now which do not contain some of her blood.

His experience of the English and Irish cross was that although, as stated, the progeny was invariably most handsome, yet it did not possess the sporting instincts and capacities of either parent. Mr. Llewellin, therefore, made further search for his ideal, and at last found it.

In 1871 he purchased, at a very high figure, the brace winners at the Shrewsbury Trials, Dick and Dan. This splendid brace of dogs was the property of Mr. Statter, Lord Derby's agent, and had been bred by him by Armstrong's Duke, of Sir V. Corbet's strain noted above, out of Rhæbe, who was nearly pure Gordon (by Gordon I do not mean black-and-tan). Mr. Llewellin discarded Dick as vastly inferior to his brother Dan, and then crossed Dan with the best pure Laverack bitches; and thus originated this celebrated breed, individuals of which speedily eclipsed, both at shows and trials, every other strain, and which still remains in its owner's hands, pure, unstained, and as good and handsome as ever.

Mr. Llewellin's strain embraces and includes all the celebrated blood of the old kennels that we have noted above, and it has only been by the most careful and scientific selection, which, of course, called for a judgment of which few men are possessed, that he has so notably succeeded. The more perfectly shaped animals were selected, and this with the greatest rigour, while all that was at all faulty was discarded. The character also and the innate proclivities of each individual were most carefully studied, and the minor faults and infirmities in one individual were corrected

95

by selecting a mate which, in those special particulars, he considered calculated to do so. In this manner Mr. Llewellin may be said to have attained the object for which he had worked for many years—viz. the combining of great beauty with surpassing field excellence. And this was abundantly proved by the practical invincibility of his strain, both in the field and on the show-bench.

Some fine specimens of this strain were exported many years since to America, where they became very celebrated, and appear to have entirely regenerated the transatlantic aboriginal. Report says, however, that in these days "the Llewellin Setter," as bred by American breeders, has greatly deteriorated. This is not remarkable, as inbreeding without the most scientific selection must always be a failure. Some people breed entirely from pedigree, irrespective of looks and performances, others entirely from looks, others again entirely from performances. Each of these methods by itself is suicidal, and must result sooner or later, and generally sooner, in the utter ruin of any breed.

The Llewellin Setter has been much used for crossing with other breeds, and would have been more so if individuals had not been so very hard to procure. Mr. Llewellin has always been very jealous of his dogs, and on several occasions has refused sums of four figures for certain individuals. Still, wherever this blood has been used, as in the kennels of Captain Lonsdale, who had some good old blood of his own, Colonel Cotes, Mr. Webber, the well-known Bishops, and others, it has had a marked effect. The most noteworthy instance of this that the writer can call to mind was in the case of Mr. Webber, who purchased, many years ago, a Llewellin puppy at Aldridge's, and mixing the blood with his own curious breed, produced such a celebrated dog as " Prince W." In the next generations, however, the principles of selection were disregarded, and the usual result appeared.

The Llewellin Setter has a peculiar character of its own which once seen is unmistakable. On more than one occasion the writer himself has identified individuals where he had no suspicion whatever that they could be present. He saw a dog once in the street of a town in the wilds of British Columbia, and spotted it at once.

The English Setter that one now sees at field trials and shows has dwindled down to a much smaller size than that of its progenitors. Mr. Llewellin's strain alone seems to have preserved, very nearly if not quite, its normal stature. Here are the measurements of a dog and a bitch at present in his possession; they are of the same litter, of unstained pedigree, and about four years old ; both have great beauty and quality, and are perfect in the field.

Dan Wind 'Em. Height at shoulder, 25⅝in. ; length from tip of nose to root of tail, 34in. ; length of head, 9in. ; girth of chest, 32¼in. ; girth of loin, 24½in.

Ruth Wind 'Em. Height, 23¼in.; length, 34in.; head, 9in.; chest, 30¼in.; loin, 24in.

Just as the appearance of the Llewellin Setter has a peculiar character, so also have its qualities in the field—there is something as unmistakable as it is indescribable in the "go" of a pure Llewellin, and the nose is quite unrivalled. The generality of the breed have an innate faculty for finding birds at immense distances and galloping up to them, that the writer has never seen in any other strain. There is also another peculiarity that he has never observed elsewhere, and only in a few specimens even of this famous breed. It is that of "spotting" birds in their range and leaving them till the next "quarter." The fact is, the nose is so sensitive that the dog detects the scent of birds an enormous way off, and its courage, at the same time, is so high that it will not condescend to go to it as yet. The writer has often watched a dog of this breed ranging at a terrific pace from hedge to hedge slightly toss his chin up at right angles to his beat, without pausing, several times; on the return range he would 'come back like a hurricane, and take up each several point as he came to it, returning often from the first some yards down wind in order to make the second, and so on.

The shape and make of a Setter should, as far as the body is concerned, be as similar as possible to that of a perfectly shaped hunter—of the long and low type; a long neck, sloping shoulder, short back, deep but not broad chest, thighs long from hip to hock, hocks straight and stifles well bent, pasterns strong and straight, and loins strong, deep, and wide. The head should be long and fairly broad. The nose should be large and straight, with a turn if anything upwards, brown in lemons and black in other colours. The nostrils should be broad and expanded, the jaws absolutely level, ears set low and hanging level with the head. The eye should be full, sparkling, and intelligent, and the colour thereof should be brown. The hare foot is the more lasting, though it is said that many people prefer the cat foot. The stern should be of moderate length, carried straight without a curl, and shaped something like a sabre. The coat should be fine, silky, soft, and straight. The high carriage of head, which is one of the most striking attributes of a perfect Setter, cannot exist without a fine, sloping shoulder.

In selecting a puppy it is important carefully to note all these points, and with this object in view, the best way is to put the puppy on a table, and so to get it nearly level with your eye. Over and above make and shape, it is very important carefully to study disposition and temperament. If you are choosing from a litter of from seven to eight weeks old, it is a good plan to get the puppies all round you in a kennel, and to observe which takes the most notice of you, and is the most intelligent and affectionate; it is also advisable

97

suddenly to stamp your foot, to light a Vesuvian with a good crack, to strike an iron-shod stick against a stone floor, or any dodge of this sort which may give you an idea as to whether there is an inclination to resent noises, and so to develop into gun-shyness.

As to the breaking, or, rather, as the writer prefers to call it, the education of the puppy, this should be taken in hand as soon as your pupil is able to walk. Habits of prompt obedience can then be cultivated easily. It should be a hard-and-fast rule that the puppy should never be allowed to roam about by itself, or to go out with anybody except its master; above all, it should never be frightened in any way, it should never be struck with the hand even, much less with a whip, for many months, and it should never be *driven* into its kennel. If its owner, too, has time and patience, it may be taught by degrees to point bits of biscuit hidden in long grass, and all that sort of thing.

Any education which has a tendency to develop brain power and to cultivate intellect as well as to promote obedience and a fellow-feeling with its master will prove most valuable, as long as trick-teaching is not overdone, and above all things as long as no severity of any sort is practised. A puppy thus brought up will more than recompense all trouble, when the age for training to game is reached.

At what age this should commence it is impossible to say. The general rule would be to begin as soon as the puppy starts to range freely, but with some young dogs it is necessary to get scent into their noses before they will begin to range at all; so that the age must be left to the intelligence of "the tutor."

Now, this tutor must not be surprised or disappointed if his pupil runs utterly wild and is apparently unmanageable when first introduced to birds. Very often the puppy which has been highly educated will be wilder to begin with than a neglected one; but there will always be this difference, the educated one will know right from wrong at the slightest hint from its master, and its disobedience will soon cease.

Some years since the writer had two beautiful Llewellin puppies which he had educated most elaborately from their earliest babyhood. When they were only about three months old they would drop well to hand, stay where they were told, follow at heel, come well to whistle, and obey all orders promptly; at a very early age, too, they were very high rangers. One day they came for the first time across a brace of birds. They chased them, one giving tongue, for a good mile, flying several fences, swimming a small river, and crossing a railway, and this in spite of all whistles and objurgations. On their return they were talked to a great deal, and had a few very mild slaps with the hand. The next day one of them stood birds well and dropped to wing, and neither was much trouble afterwards. The reason was, simply, they quite understood what they had done wrong, and had no desire, that they were unable to restrain, to displease their master by repeating the offence.

There is plenty of rule-of-thumb dog-breaking done with a thick whip and a loud voice; but this sort of breaking ruins far more dogs than it renders useful. There is no science in the world which requires more intellect, judgment, and discrimination than the *real education* of sporting dogs.

FIG. 58.—MR. PURCELL LLEWELLIN'S ENGLISH SETTER DAN.

It is hard to prophesy as to the future of the Setter, but the writer must confess that he has great misgivings. As long as Setter men are divided, as now, into two classes—the show-bench men, who are content with a certain beauty of form which attracts the judge, but which in many respects is inconsistent with field work, and the field-trial man, who does not care if his dog is as ugly as a pig as long as it can win—it is a bad look-out. There are several very large field-trial kennels in England at the present time, but their owners, as a rule, do not breed on any system; far oftener will they purchase any winner, with little or no regard to looks or pedigree, and then breed from it with no science or discrimination.

The original object of dog shows—*i.e.* as far as sporting dogs are concerned—was of course to promote and preserve in the greatest possible perfection the properties and attributes, as well as the form-beauty, of the various breeds used in the field, and for some years after their first establishment this most laudable and useful purpose was to a great extent accomplished. At that time, however, it must be remembered that the animals shown were invariably used for shooting, and also that the judges were always sportsmen. It naturally followed, therefore, that although the prize winners were not necessarily superior in their field work, but sometimes even inferior to the dogs which were passed over, still, the winners must have had *some* merit in their special province, or they would not have remained in existence. Now all this is changed; dog shows have become a medium for money-making, and so the breeding of sporting dogs (so called) has become a regular business in itself and entirely divorced from the proper use of the animal.

Where, twenty-five years ago, there was one show, there are now one hundred ; where three prizes at most were given for one particular breed, there are now a dozen or more, and the merits of the winners are thus complicated and lessened. The judges, too, are not invariably sportsmen ; it is even probable that some of them have never seen the work of a Setter or a Pointer in their lives. How, then, is it possible for them to know that that dog of beautiful *quality* to which they give a first prize has shoulders so loaded that he could not gallop for an hour, or quarters so short or so weak that he could never get to the top of a high hill at all ? There seems also to be no standard for size, so the Setter gets smaller every year. Again, how can it be *expected* that the modern show Setter can be anything but useless in "the field" ? He spends nearly the whole of his time in a hamper or on a show-bench ; he is fed on stimulating food, kept in warm kennels, and washed and brushed and combed and pampered. What chance *can* he ever have of cultivating or even preserving the sporting instincts of his *far-away* progenitors—far away indeed, for it must be remembered that this dog showing has been going on now for many canine generations. Of course it must stand to reason that the dog should lose altogether the sporting faculties of his forbears ; and the worst of it is, nobody cares a cent whether he does or not !

The show-bench winner in the seventies and early eighties may be defined as the most refined member of a family of well-formed and keen, intelligent working Setters.

Now it presents a type peculiar to itself—a heavier type more after that of the Clumber Spaniel. It is clean cut and well formed, in head and ears and throat, and has a good coat. It is, however, very deficient in hindquarters, and has a dull, apathetic, soft, unintelligent air, betokening a want of constitution begotten by the unnatural existence of shows, instead of the natural and invigorating life of the moors and fields.

Between the Show and the Field Setter there *ought* of course to be no difference ; on the contrary, the show should help the sportsman to preserve in their fullest perfection the shape, the make, the attributes which are positively necessary for the proper performance of the field duties of his canine assistants.

Mr. Llewellin has preserved his peculiar blend of Setter blood

FIG. 59.—MR. PURCELL LLEWELLIN'S ENGLISH SETTER COUNTESS.

during thirty-two years absolutely intact from any outside admixture whatever ; and we can trace back the pedigrees thereof for more than a century. He is therefore the only man living at the present time who can be said to possess a positively pure and unmixed strain of this beautiful dog.   .

The illustrations, Figs. 58, 59, and 60, are of great interest ; they serve as an object-lesson of Mr. Llewellin's work. First we have Dan, representing one line of his blood—viz. a combination of the Gordon and Southesk strains ; secondly, Countess, a pure Laverack of the Dash and Moll family, and perhaps the most beautiful and the truest-shaped bitch of her day ; thirdly, Countess Bear, by Dan ex Countess. Here we have the result of the combination of these two lines ; this animal, which shows the size of the Dan line and commanding a full view of the beaten ground, and was regaling himself with divers sandwiches, when he noticed a black-and-white dog ranging the exact country he had been carefully beating, and of course thought at first that it was some rival sportsman who was ignorantly traversing the same ground. He looked and looked, but could see no *man*, and at last it struck him that the dog must be hunting him. By-and-by, as the dog topped a gate about half a mile below, the writer recognised the Setter Grouse. It was a most interesting thing to watch, as from that point he had made several wide detours in pursuit of marked birds and to beat likely fields, and so on. When the dog lost his scent he would make a wide cast like a hound and recover it, and at times, as in ploughed fields, would plod on the scent at a walk. At last he got into the big grass field where he was sitting, and with head up and stern down raced into him.

It appeared afterwards that his master thought that he would go out for a quiet shoot about noon, and loosed his dog. Grouse never even looked at him, but taking up the writer's five hours ago trail on the road, ran it at a great pace until finding him as he has described. Needless to say, the writer bought the dog and shot over him many seasons, and a most wonderful animal he turned out.

In woods, as well as in the open, the dog was first rate ; in a wood he would range right away out of sight, and the writer used to saunter along at his ease with a very clever Retriever at heel. If in the course of a few minutes Grouse did not appear on his return quarter, one whistle would be given, and if he did not come then, the Retriever was told to find him. She would at once follow his trail slowly, looking back and waiting for her master at intervals, till at last she would suddenly back, and there the old boy would be, standing as stiff as a rock, and by hook or by crook the two dogs and the man would generally secure the object of attraction. If, again, one was working a river for water-fowl, the dog would take the opposite bank, if so directed, and point anything he came across, waiting until the Retriever swam over to put it up ; he would never put it up himself or chase it when she did, but sit down and watch quietly what took place, and after the gun was loaded and the thing retrieved, he would continue the even tenour of his way. On several occasions, too, when he saw wild ducks on the water he would drop and hide himself and leave his master to stalk them, or, if he thought it could be done, he would make a circuit as quick as lightning, get in front of the ducks and jump into the water, barking furiously, and the ducks would thus frequently come right over the snug place where the writer had concealed himself when he had noticed the dog's tactics.

Another very clever Setter was owned by the writer when living in America for a few years. She was given to him as a puppy, made a great pet of, and was nearly always his constant companion. Not having another dog, he taught her to retrieve, which she would do perfectly both by land and water. For the ordinary prairie chicken and willow grouse work she became very perfect, and was so untiring that she would frequently accompany him on his rides of sixty to eighty miles, ranging the prairies for long distances while his horse pursued his even course along "the trail." The writer always carried a gun strapped to the saddle in a thick cover, and his saddle-bags were often full of game when he arrived at his destination.

One evening he was returning home after a long, wearying ride, and it was just getting dusk when he missed the dog. He whistled for some time and was getting uneasy, when she appeared, in a great hurry. He was riding on, when she ran in front of the horse, and stood pointing dead at him. He pulled up and said, " What's up, old girl? Go on and tell me." She raced back in great glee, and, pointing at intervals to let him keep up, went back along the trail for a quarter of a mile, and then going into some bush on the right, stood like a statue. He was off in a moment, got a right and left at a lot of chickens, marked the rest down, luckily on the road home, and got six more of them to single points. Ever after that she never failed to carry out the plan that she had invented and had found so successful. She would range away a mile or more out of sight as her master was travelling, suddenly appear, in a great hurry, and then lead him back to some game she had found and left in order to fetch him. She would do more than this. Prairie chicken very frequently lie in belts of a willow called cotton-wood, and it is very difficult, if one is alone, to get a shot at them. This dog, after making a point in a place of this sort, would turn round, sit down, and look at her master; having thus indicated what to expect, she would make a wide circuit in the wood and get in front of the birds, which usually run away from a dog, quietly and calmly like turkeys, she would head them, "round them up" when they required it, and, pointing and drawing, would drive them quietly out exactly to the spot where her master was concealed. She very often got the whole lot thus into the open, and then would stand and look round for him; thus, of course, it was easy to get one's shot and very often to mark the covey down again. It did not, however, much matter about this latter, as if she once knew the direction which birds had taken, she was bound to find them again if you would let her, as she would go on hunting for miles in wide circles till she did.

She got cleverer and cleverer at this game as time went on, until at last she became the most "killing" dog to shoot to that it was possible to have.

The following incident in her career corroborated to a great extent a favourite theory that the writer has long held—viz. that when a dog's *intellect* is cultivated, he is fully capable, if no obstacle is put in his way, of the further cultivation of it himself almost to any extent.

One day the writer was out shooting with this bitch, accompanied by one friend, in a very hard frost. There was hardly any scent of course, but she managed, with very great caution, to find several grouse at short distances. We had just arrived at the corner of a copse of willows, at the bottom of which was a river. Belle, who was soberly trotting a few yards in front of us, suddenly stopped, pointed for a second towards the wood, then looked round, and scurried away down the outside as fast as she could go. Without a word being spoken, we drew behind a tree and waited. We saw the bitch disappear in the wood close to the river, and then there was silence for a few minutes. Of course we thought that she was after her old dodge of driving grouse to the gun. By-and-by there was a mighty crashing in the interior of the copse, accompanied, to our utter bewilderment, by a furious barking, and then within five yards of us there emerged two deer, with Belle close behind them. We were, alas! only charged with shot, so we contented ourselves with shooting at one only, and our four barrels stopped him in a few hundred yards.

Here is another instance of intelligent reasoning. The writer was shooting alone with a Setter and a Retriever on a Cornish moor, when a woodcock rose in a bit of brush. It was an awkward shot between the trees, and he went on apparently unhurt. Now, there was a narrow belt of thin wood on the left hand and a marsh below, and the Setter took the two in her range. The writer noticed that she stopped for a moment at one place in the brushwood, but thought nothing of it. A couple of hundred yards or so farther she pointed a snipe, which was killed. As the Retriever was coming up with it, the Setter looked at the writer from her down charge with a most quizzical gaze, and then got up and ran back as hard as she could pelt. The old Retriever, standing still with the snipe in her mouth, looked at her with wonder. Away she went out of sight, and in a few seconds came tearing back, spit a woodcock out at the writer's feet with awful disgust, and then went on hunting. There seems to be no doubt that, seeing the Retriever bring the snipe made her think she ought to have done the same with the dead thing she had seen and left back in the brush, and that she at once proceeded to atone for the omission.

The following shows also a natural reasoning power in a Setter, even when it had not been cultivated. He was a Llewellin, and good, though not nearly as good as the generality of that strain—in fact, his education had been neglected : he had just been " broken," and nothing more. He did not seem to have any "gumption" about anything, would go down wind just as fast as up, and of course put up birds by the score. Whenever therefore the writer went into a field down wind, he always took him up till he got the full breeze in his face. This was done for a few days, and the dog improved very much. One afternoon, having to beat a very long, narrow piece of roots, the writer would not take the trouble of going to the end, but went in down wind and let the dog go. He immediately went to the hedge and along it to the top of the field, and then beat it in perfect form back up wind, and after that he never failed to do the same thing.

As showing what extraordinary noses some of these Llewellins have, here are two instances of two different dogs, both on grouse. The first was a puppy in his first season, a tremendous galloper and carrying a very high head. The writer was beating a gently sloping open moor, on the left were three or four large hillocks, and on these and their surroundings the heather had been burned. The dog was ranging well ahead of the gun and taking quarters of about half a mile in length, when suddenly throwing up his head higher than one would have thought any dog could get it, he raced to the top of one of these bare hillocks and there stood like a tower. In front of him there was bare, burnt ground for at least a hundred yards. "Hare gone away, sur," said the keeper. "Hare be blowed!" was the writer's reply. Walking up to the dog, he drew him on and on and on, no tracks or signs of grouse being visible. Now he becomes perfectly rigid, and up gets a covey of about thirty under his nose. The keeper stepped the distance to where the dog first stood on the hillock, and it was 401yds. The birds, of course, *might* have run, but they certainly did not run those first hundred yards of bare ground, and the rest was very *thick* heather.

The second instance was also with a young dog, who had been well shot over for the first month on a Scotch moor. Grouse were now few and wild, and the writer wanted to get some photos of two of the dogs on point. A gun was carried just to encourage them. By-and-by one of them comes to a fine point, and (we had had a very long walk to get it) he was photographed in due form. Now, it was rather a mean thing to do, but we wanted to save time, so a lead was put on the pointing dog, and the other behind him was enlarged. This also was a particularly good-nosed dog. He galloped on into the wind and never made a sign; after giving him several casts, he was taken up and the first again enlarged. Once more he at once made the point, and putting a handkerchief down to mark the place, the writer drew him on for 103yds., where lay a grouse stone dead and nearly cold that had been killed by a hawk.

There are some Setters, too, that have the extraordinary faculty of going up to game in a field without beating any other part of the said field. The most remarkable instance of this seen by the writer was as follows : We had been shooting a wild manor where birds were very scarce, and had beaten a certain turnip-field with good cover twice already, and killed several things in it. Immediately after leaving this field for the second time three single birds were marked back into it. The Llewellin bitch the writer was working was a well-known clipper, and it was not worth while to go to the end of the field to get the wind, so he let her go clean down wind. She went straight to the end of the field, threw up her head, galloped a hundred yards or so, and dropped. That was bird No. 1. Then in a straight line to the second and in like manner to the third. All three having been slain, she took one sniff of the wind, and then sauntered calmly up a drill and lay down to await us at the gate.

A whole volume might be filled with anecdotes such as these as to the intelligence, the genius, and general character of the Setter.

What a pity it seems that it is considered better "form" nowadays to stand shivering in a butt or under a hedge and slaying hecatombs of driven game than to watch the surpassing genius of the dog, exercised for our sake to provide us with real, genuine sport. Ah! "the old order" has passed away, never to return. "*Sic transit gloria mundi!*"

The English Setter

MOST authorities, or those who have made diligent inquiries into the history—if such it can be called—or origin, of the English Setter, are agreed that it has been derived from the Spaniel—Setting Spaniel—and Laverack, in his work on the Setter, says,—

"I am of the opinion that all Setters have more or less originally sprung from our various strains of Spaniels, and I believe most breeders of any note agree that the Setter is nothing more than a Setting Spaniel. How the Setter attained his sufficiency of point is difficult to account for, and I leave the question to wiser heads than mine to determine. The Setter is said and acknowledged by authorities of long standing, to be of greater antiquity than the Pointer. If this be true—and I believe it is—the Setter cannot at first have been crossed with the Pointer to render him what he is."

If the foregoing views be accepted, it follows that our lovely Setter is but an improved Spaniel.

The Laverack Setters—a strain preserved by the

A Brace of English Setters at Repose (Pride and Sally, Mr Stanhope Lovell).

An English Setter (Romney Rock).

late Mr Laverack—has always played an important part in the more recent history of the Setter. The Llewellin Setter—a strain bred by Mr Llewellin —(a Laverack cross) stands out as being one of the best strains ever produced, both on the show bench and in the field.

A high-class English Setter should have a rich, glossy coat, and every movement should be one of elegance, dash, and beauty.

A high degree of intelligence and great power of physical endurance are a *sine qua non*.

Field trials have done more towards perfecting the working qualities of the Setter than could have been attained by any other means.

The breeding of stock from dogs coming out top at these trials affords the surest means of attaining the highest degree of working capacity.

The points of the English Setter are as follows :—

Coat.—To be soft, silky, and free from curl. There ought to be an abundance of soft feather on fore and hind legs.

Colour.—Not a great deal of importance is attached to this. The chief colours are :—Liver and white, lemon and white, black, black and white, red or yellow, orange Belton, black and white ticked, with splashes of black, or bluish tint—blue Belton, black, white and tan markings, &c. Black and white ticked are commonest.

Skull.—Long and narrow, with a well-developed occipital bone. Muzzle square, and lips full at their angles.

Ears and Eyes.—Ears set on low, thin and soft, carried close to the cheeks, and covered by silky hair about a couple of inches in length. Eyes of medium size, either brown or hazel.

Neck.—Slightly arched and covered by somewhat loose skin.

Back and Quarters.—Arched, and loins wide and strong. Hocks, strong.

Tail.—Should be carried in a straight line with the body, and the feather upon it to consist of straight, silky hairs, shortening towards the point. A beautiful flag is a great adornment to the Setter, especially when at work.

Fore-limbs.—Shoulders set well back. Forearms straight and strong, of medium length, and with a good fringe at the back. Pasterns short and nearly vertical. Feet well feathered below and cat-like.

Weight.—Dogs from 50 to 60 lbs. Bitches, 45 to 55 lbs. *Club.*—The English Setter.

Faults.—Curly coat, snipy head, bad carriage of stern, too light in bone, too short or too long in leg, out at elbows, too heavy in head, bad symmetry, disobedience, bad scenting power, indifferent at work, etc., etc.

The English Setter

N the preliminary history of the spaniels we expressed the opinion that although the pointer had been the recognised dog for use with the gun before the setter became his rival, there was no doubt that many sportsmen made use of setters to shoot over, preferring that dog, even if it was hardly considered correct, and from these beginnings the dog speedily became as prominent a gun dog as the pointer. We may assume that this growth of the setter began about 1775 and by 1800 was fully established, and that at the latter period there were not only the setters developed from the setting spaniel by gentlemen who took pride in their kennels, but plenty of half-bred setters and pointers, droppers as they were called, and also that almost any spaniel, so long as he was a good working dog, was used by men who cared little about good looks or type and wanted something useful.

That state of affairs is to be found as preliminary to the establishment of all breeds and the meeting of rivals in competition for judgment. As illustrative of this we need not do more than look at the first volume of the Stud Book issued in 1879 by the National American Kennel Club, not the present ruling body but one more interested in field trials than in dogs in general. This volume contains the registrations of fourteen hundred dogs, of which 533 are English setters of pure breeding; 260 Irish setters, also pure, and 135 Gordon setters; pointers number 165, while 65 spaniels of various kinds and Chesapeake Bay dogs make up the total. In this volume there is a division for "Cross-bred and other Setters," at the head of which there is this note of explanation: "Owing to the indefinite character of some pedigrees it was impossible to decide to what breed certain dogs belonged. They are therefore included in the present class, under the head of 'Other Setters' to save discarding them altogether. In this section there are no fewer than 260 entries. And these were not dogs owned by a lot of nobodies, but by men of recognised position in the sporting-dog world, such names as Jesse Sherwood, James Smith, C. T. Prince, G. C. Colburn, A. C. Waddell, Von Culin, and Everett Smith appearing on the first two pages, and as we glance further we note such leaders' names as Wm. M. Tileston, Dr. J. S. Niven, Major J. M. Taylor (with a tricombination of English, Gordon and Irish bred by the enthusiast of the Laverack importations, Mr. Charles H. Raymond), Dr. Aten of Brooklyn, E. F. Stoddard of Dayton, George B. Raymond of Morris Plains, George Bird Grinnell, T. Foreman Taylor, Edward Dexter, Garret Roach, H. C. Glover, E. A. Spooner, Wm. Tallman, Leslie C. Bruce, Justus von Lengerke, Isaac Fiske, J. H. Whitman, Jacob Glahn of Syracuse, and many others better known only to the older generation of setter men than those we have picked out. It would be impossible to imagine any of the above-named gentlemen, who are still living, owning anything nowadays but of the purest breeding possible, yet we copy from the records of but twenty-five years ago."

With such evidence of mixed breeding in this country when so much was known regarding the higher breeding of the setter abroad, and when not only some of the choicest of the Laveracks had been here for some four or five years, but Leicester, Dart, Rock and a whole host of the "blue bloods" subsequently styled "Llewellyns" were spread about the country, can we imagine anything else of England one hundred years ago than that here and there was something akin to fancy breeding, that is, with an eye to certain characteristics, while the majority indulged in cross-breeding quite regardless of looks or type? It stands to reason that such was the case, and it is therefore only what is to be expected when we come to read the only book which is really historical, "The Setter, by Edward Laverack." His knowledge of the Setter dated from early in the last century, for he went shooting in the Highlands when he was eighteen and in his introduction he acknowledges to being seventy-three years of age, while the date of the book is 1872, hence he must have had personal knowledge of setters from about 1815, and his statements are exactly in keeping with this very natural conclusion of what must have been the case.

It is only proper, however, to take authors a little more chronologically and we will begin with Daniels's "Rural Sports," published at the beginning of the nineteenth century. From the references to this book in later publications one would infer that it contained a most valuable contribution to dog history, but such is far from being the case, and what he says is without practical value. What is valuable, however, is that it contains three

THE GAMEKEEPER

By Stubbs, in Daniel's "Rural Sports," 1802

THE ENGLISH SETTER

By Reinagle, in Scott's "Sportsman's Repository," 1820

114

engravings from paintings of setters by different artists. The one by Reinagle shows a beautiful dog, much handsomer and of a great deal more quality than the same artist's setter in the "Sportman's Repository," of twenty-five years later. The very extraordinary setter accompanying the game-keeper is a painting by G. Stubbs, a very famous animal artist.

We now take up the actual history of the making of the English setter, and we are not only indebted for all pertinent information on the subject to the late Edward Laverack, but above that we are most unquestionably indebted to him for placing the setter in its proper position as a field dog and for the development of the type which was not only the standard of excellence in his day, but that upon which we have built the present-day setter. For some peculiar reason it has been the custom of a certain class of writers to belittle Mr. Laverack and what he accomplished, alleging that the inconsistencies in his statements regarding the pedigrees of his dogs and some such small matters condemned the whole business. If Mr. Laverack had never given a single pedigree with any of his dogs, and had never told any person how they were bred, they would have been just as good workers, just as good looking and in every way as useful in building up the breed. As a strain they were unequalled in their day, and but for them Americans would have had poor material in the way of importations with which to improve the natives of inter-variety breeding. Strangest of all, most of those who attacked Mr. Laverack and his dogs were thick-and-thin supporters of what has been named the "Llewellyn" setter, a strain made up from dogs bought, not bred, by Mr. Purcell Llewellyn, one-half of the desired pedigree being Laverack blood. On this subject we will have more to say later.

But for Mr. Laverack we should know nothing of the various strains kept by sporting gentlemen of prominence throughout England and Scotland, and in his book, "The Setter," is to be found all that later writers knew about the various strains and which they made use of without compunction as original. Mr. Laverack's book is now exceedingly scarce, almost, if not quite, as hard to secure as the first edition of "Stonehenge," which many have thought did not exist. As Mr. Laverack's text is condensed it may be copied in full, so far as reference is made to the leading varieties of the English setter from the time his knowledge of them began, which we may set down as 1815-20.

Naworth Castle or Featherstone Castle Setters

The first he mentions is the Naworth Castle or Featherstone Castle setters: "There is a very fine old breed of setters, at present but little known. It has been, and still is, in the possession of the Earl of Carlisle, Naworth Castle, Brampton, Cumberland; Lord Wallace, Featherstone Castle, Cumberland, and Major Cowan, of Blaydon Burn, Northumberland, so well known as the bloodhound authority.

"This breed of setters I remember fifty years ago, when I rented the moors belonging to the Earl of Carlisle, in the vicinity of Gillesland. This moor was commonly called Wastes, a description of which is so graphically given by Sir Walter Scott in 'Guy Mannering.'

"This rare old breed has probably been retained in the above families as long as any other strain has.

"The Featherstone Castle breed has been looked after by three generations of Prouds, Edward Proud (now pensioned off) and sons.

"Those at Naworth Castle, by Grisdale, who has been there for forty years or more, but now a pensioner. How long the breed may have been in the family of Major Cowan, and others in Northumberland and Cumberland I cannot say.

"The distinguishing colour is liver and white, they are very powerful in the chest, deep and broad, not narrow or slaty, which some people seem to think is the true formation of the setter.

"If there is any fault to find with them it is their size; they are a little too big and heavy.

"There is a great profusion of coat, of a light, soft silky hair on the crest of the head, which is rather longer and heavier than the generality of setters. They are particularly strong and powerful in their fore quarters, beautifully feathered on their fore legs, tail and breeches, easily broken, very lofty in their carriage, staunch, excellent dogs and good finders. Though liver, or liver and white is not a recognised colour in shows, my belief is that there are as good dogs of this colour as of any other.

"The Featherstone Castle breed was brought into notoriety by the late keeper, Edward Proud, and so much were they appreciated by shooting men that they went all over the country, and even to Ireland. This was more than half a century ago.

THE SETTER
By Reinagle in Daniels' " Rural Sports," 1802

THE OLD ENGLISH SETTER
From Daniels' " Rural Sports," 1802

"There is also another celebrated breed at Edmond Castle, near Carlisle, Cumberland. This likewise is liver and white, without the tuft. These dogs are much lighter and more speedy looking than the tufted ones. They are very deep, wide and powerful in the forequarters; well bent in the stifles, so much so as to give them a cat-like crouching attitude.

"Laidlaw was the keeper's name who had charge of them. These setters were noted all over the country for being first class and very enduring.

"The late Mr. Heythorn, of Melmerby Hall, near Penrith, had this breed when he shot with me—at which time I had the shooting at Pitmain, Kingussie, Inverness-shire—and first-rate dogs they were.

"Mr. Garth's Bess, a winner at the Shrewsbury trials, was from this kennel."

How far the following strains, which Mr. Laverack refers to, resembled what we call black, white and tan, or how nearly they favoured Gordons with white markings, we have no means of stating, but are inclined to the opinion that they were distinct from the latter, for the reason that Mr. Laverack put them in one chapter, devoting the following chapter to the Gordon, or black and tan alone, then a chapter to his own breed, finishing with another devoted to the Irish setter. This seems conclusive evidence that he did not consider them allied to the Gordons, but as varieties of the general run of setters.

Lord Lovat's Breed

Lord Lovat's breed is named as a black, white and tan: "Another celebrated, tested and well-known breed has long been in the possession of the evergreen veteran sportsman, Lord Lovat, Beaufort Castle, Beauly, Inverness-shire. This strain is black, white and tan. His Lordship shot long with Alexander, the late Duke of Gordon, and he informed me that his Grace had black and tans, and black, white and tans, but preferred the latter.

"A celebrated dog of Lord Lovat's black, white and tan named Regent was well known in Ross-shire and Inverness-shire. Old Bruce, his Lordship's keeper, told me this dog would never be beaten. Numbers of this strain and colour were in Lord Lovat's kennels when I last saw them. They have long been valued by many sportsmen for their excellence and beauty.

118

"I think I am correct in stating that this breed has never been exhibited at dog shows. They are very handsome, good, possessed of great powers of endurance; kept for utility and not for show.

THE SOUTHESK

"There is also another breed called the Southesk, belonging to the Earl of Southesk, in Forfarshire, black, white and tan. These dogs are very strong, fine animals, large in size and extremely well feathered, round barrelled, powerful, and strong in their forequarters.

"If any defect in their formation, they are apt to be somewhat slack in the loins and too long in the leg; notwithstanding this, they are well known to be good and staunch dogs, and highly appreciated.

"The breed was well known to me when I rented the forest of Birse, adjoining the Glen of Dye, the property of Sir James Carnegie, now the Earl of Southesk."

STRAINS OF THE EARL OF SEAFIELD

The Earl of Seafield had tricolours and also lemon or orange and whites. "This is one of the most beautiful strains I have ever seen; there are few better than that of the Earl of Seafield of Balmacaan, Urquhart Castle, Inverness-shire. Perhaps there is no breed of setters possessed of a greater profusion of coat. I should say, save Russians; they had more coat of a glossy, silky texture, and more feather than any other strain of setters I have ever seen. Sheriff Tytler, of Aldoury, near Inverness, also had or has some of the same breed, as well as the late General Porter of Inchnacardoch, near Fort Augustus, and several others in that district.

"I had many opportunities of seeing this pure and beautiful breed when I rented the Dunmaglass shootings and Boleskin Cottage on the banks of Loch Ness, Inverness. The formation of these dogs is as follows: Head rather short and light, full hazel eyes, ears well set on, of a soft, silky texture. They are similar to Toy Spaniels on a large scale, and covered with long floss like silky hair on body, and forelegs, flag, and breech; medium sized; good hunters; good dispositions and easily broken. The objectionable points are their peculiarly upright shoulders, straight hindquarters and sparseness of body, which makes them go short and stilty."

119

Breed of the Earl of Derby and Lord Ossulston

"The late Earl of Derby and Lord Ossulston, when shooting at Coulnakyle, in Strathspey, Inverness-shire, had a beautiful breed of lemon and white setters, obtained, I believe, from Lord Anson. This breed in formation was very similar to my own lemon and white; they were very powerful in the fore-quarters and remarkably handsome."

Lord Ossulston's Black Setters

We now return to the Border sportsmen for particulars regarding black setters: "Another breed of rare excellence, and greatly appreciated by practical sportsmen was that of Lord Ossulston, Chillingham Castle, Wooler, Northumberland. These were jet black, with beautiful bright, soft, glossy coats—a colour that our fastidious judges of the present day would probably ignore and not even notice, however handsome they might be, as not being fashionable. It was certainly one of the best, most useful and beautiful strains I ever saw, and for downright hard work could not be surpassed. I have, too, seen an excellent breed of light fawns, also a self-liver coloured one. Both these strains are first rate.

Breeds of Lord Hume, Wilson Patten and Henry Rothwell

"Lord Hume, of Tweedside; Wilson Patten, Lancashire; and the late Henry Rothwell (that celebrated old sportsman of hunting notoriety, who resided near Kendal, Westmoreland) had also a similar breed of blacks, well known, and eagerly sought after in those days by all the leading sportsmen in that country.

"Lord Hume's strain was famous all through that district and the Lammermuir Hills, for their acknowledged good properties, stoutness and powers of endurance. The last of this beautiful breed, so far as Harry Rothwell was concerned, was a dog named Paris, in the possession of his nephew, Robert Thompson, Esq., Inglewood Bank, near Penrith, Northumberland, and who shot with me for several years on the Forse shootings, Caithness, which I rented. It is a fact that this dog, a medium-sized one, ran almost every day for six weeks and he was, when required, as good a retriever as I ever saw. Mr. Ellis, the Court Lodge, near Yalding, Kent, who shot with us can testify to the truth of this statement.

"Wilson Patten's breed, similar to the above, were very good, and noted for their hardy constitutions and innate love of hard work.

"The colour of Lord Hume's and the other of the named gentlemen's breeds was a most beautiful jet black, as bright and brilliant as the blackest satin. Long, low dogs, with light heads, very strong and powerful in the forehand; well-bent, ragged, cat-like hind quarters, capital feet, hare footed, but not too much arched at the toe. They had not a great profusion of coat, but what there was, was of a first rate quality, and particularly silky.

"These dogs were exceedingly close and compact in their build, and noted all through the country for their endurance; they were good rangers and very staunch."

MR. LORT'S SETTERS

Of Mr. Lort's setters Mr. Laverack does not speak from personal knowledge, but from information he believed that there were none better. In colour they were black and white, and lemon and white; long, silky coats; hardy, enduring and good rangers. Mr. Laverack expressed his regret that owing to Mr. Lort's judging so constantly at shows, he seldom exhibited, and his setters were not known as they should have been.

THE WELSH OR LLANIDLOES SETTER

Finally we have references to the Welsh setters, of which the Llanidloes strain was then dying out. A close, compact animal, very handsome; milk-white or chalk-white, as it was called in Wales, and the coats not so soft and silky as the other breeds named. Another black strain is mentioned as equally good, hardy and enduring. "In their own country they cannot be beaten, being exactly what is required for the steep hill sides." It will be well to supplement with the late Mr. Lort's description in the "Book of the Dog" this scanty reference to the Welsh setters.

"The coat of the Welsh or Llanidloes setter, or at all events of pure bred ones, is as curly as the jacket of a Cotswold sheep, and not only is it curly, but it is hard in texture and as unlike that of a modern fashionable setter as it is possible to imagine. The colour is usually white, with occasionally a lemon coloured patch or two about the head and ears. Many

121

MR. EDWARD LAVERACK'S ENGLISH SETTER, FRED IV, BY DASH OUT OF MOLL
Drawn when 15 months of age

MR. EDWARD LAVERACK'S "OLD BLUE" DASH, BY STING OUT OF CORA
Drawn when 10 years of age

however, are pure white, and it is not unusual to find several whelps in every litter possessed of one or two pearl eyes. Their heads are longer in proportion to their size, and not so refined looking as those of the English setter. Sterns are curly and clubbed; with no fringe to them, and the tail swells out in shape something like an otter's. This breed is more useful than any spaniel, for it is smart, handy, with an excellent nose and can find with tolerable certainty at the moderate pace it goes. It usually has the habit of beating close to you, and is not too fast, being particularly clever with cocks and snipe, which they are no more likely to miss than is a spaniel."

The Laveracks and Their Breeding

It is very unfortunate that Mr. Laverack confines his comments on his own strain to a mere description of their general appearance, or what he aimed at in his breeding, and gives us no details as how he started the strain or how he progressed. He illustrates his book with likenesses of Old Blue Dash, Dash II., and Fred. IV. It is very tantalizing after reading about the other strains to find nothing about the one we desire most of all to learn how it was built up. What we do know on this score is that in 1825 he obtained from the Reverend A. Harrison, who resided near Carlisle, two setters, Ponto and Old Moll, and to these two dogs alone he traced back the Laverack setters. Mr. Harrison had kept his strain for thirty-five years and carefully guarded their breeding all that time, so that accepting the pedigrees of the Laveracks of 1870-80 as correct, the breed was in existence for nigh upon one hundred years. Mr. Laverack mentions Mr. Harrison but once, when, in naming the three most perfect setters he had ever seen, he selected Lord Lovat's black, white and tan dog Regent, General Wyndham's Irish setter, not named, and Rev. A. Harrison's Old Moll.

It has been claimed that this tracing back to these two dogs alone is fundamentally wrong and that Mr. Laverack brought outside blood into his strain, and as evidence of this there is a letter he wrote his friend Rothwell regarding a puppy that was liver and white saying: "The liver and white will be quite as handsome and good as any of the five in the litter. He strains back to Prince's sire, viz., Pride of the Border, a liver and white. He strains back for thirty years to a change of blood I once introduced—the pure old Edward Castle breed—County Cumberland liver and white, quite as pure and as good as the blues. Pride's dam was my old blue and white, with tan cheeks and eyebrows. Why I reserved Pride was to breed back with him and my blues. He is invaluable as by him I can carry on the breed." This was written in May, 1874, two years later than the book was published, and of course is a contradiction of the pedigree he gave with that dog and every other by Dash II. out of Belle II., and indeed of all his pedigrees, for if one goes they all go, so similar are they in the interbreeding of the descendants of these two original dogs he started with. So on this allegation those opposed to the Laveracks attacked the whole structure, root and branch. But what was there in that after all? Did the excellence of the Laveracks depend upon whether or not all Mr. Laverack's self-acknowledged tests to improve his strain were subsequently, as he said elsewhere, thrown out, or whether some mixture of some excellent blood still remained, or did their claims rest upon what they were individually? Were they not the outcome of fifty years of his own breeding with a well-defined object in view? These are the points at issue and nothing else, except with that class of breeders who select a sire from the stud-book record of pedigrees—and never breed anything good for either show or field trials.

We are far from supporting the published Laverack pedigrees—quite the reverse, in fact, for it is simply impossible that that of Countess is correct. If that one falls, they all go, at least all with any such cross as Dash II.—or Old Blue Dash as he was generally called—or that of Fred I. Usually the Laverack pedigrees are attacked upon two grounds, the presumed impossibility for any strain to have its origin in but one brace of dogs and to interbreed their progeny successfully for fifty years. The other claim is that as Mr. Laverack tried some outcrosses and never gave a pedigree with such a cross in it, coupled with the statement with regard to the liver colour in Pride of the Border, he did not give correct pedigrees. There is no foundation for the first assumption as it would be quite possible to continue the interbreeding of descendants from one brace of dogs, exercising care to breed only from the physically sound ones. With regard to the second claim we will say, presuming that nothing further can be adduced against the given pedigrees, that a person writing an offhand reply to an intimate friend would hardly exercise the care nor make the necessary references he would if writing out a pedigree for publication. We would not take the Rothwell letter as conclusive against the testimony of the pedigree if the latter bore investigation, and that leads us to a line of discussion which we

MR. C. H. RAYMOND'S CHAMPION PRIDE OF THE BORDER
A leader in the early Laverack importations

LEICESTER   *Photo by Schreiber*
One of the earliest importations from Mr. Purcell-Llewellyn's kennels by Mr. L. H. Smith, of Strathroy, Canada

have not hitherto seen exploited, though it may possibly have been without our knowledge.

Mr. Laverack obtained Ponto and Old Moll from the Rev A. Harrison in 1825. Judging from Mr. Laverack's naming Old Moll, coupled with the name of Mr. Harrison, as one of the best three setters he had known, it would seem fair to assume that he did not get her as a puppy, but probably obtained both as developed shooting dogs, having possibly no thought of what he subsequently went in for in breeding. We will therefore set the date of their birth at 1823. The peculiarity in the pedigree of Countess is not really so much that all lines trace back to the original brace, but that the links are so few and each brace named has but two descendants, with but two exceptions of one additional each. Boiled down in this manner here is the pedigree of Countess:

Main stem.   Spurs—see below.

(1823) Ponto—Old Moll.
     ¹Dash I.—Belle I.
     Pilot—²Moll II.   ³Cora I.
     Regent—Jet I.   ⁴Rock.
     Rock II.—Blairs Cora.
     ⁵Sting — ⁶Belle II.
        sire of   dam of
(1862) Dash II.   Moll III.
        Countess (1869)

Spurs to the main line:

         ¹Dash I.   ²Moll II. (? 1836)

      ⁴Rock   Peg

       Rock I.

   ⁶Belle II.   Fred I. (1853)   ³Cora I. (? 1836)

     Moll III.   Cora II.   ⁵Sting.

                  Dash II. (1862)

       Countess (1869)

Referring to the main stem table, we have six generations from Ponto to Dash II., a period of thirty-nine years, or an average of six and a half years to a generation. According to that supposition Moll II. and Cora I. were whelped about 1836. Turning to the table of spurs, we have Fred I. recorded as whelped in 1853, by which time his dam, Moll II. was, according to the foregoing computation, seventeen years old. We next come to a veritable Sarah in brood bitches, the venerable Cora I. a full sister, possibly a litter sister to Moll II., and find that she was bred to this nephew of hers, Fred I., about 1857, and when about twenty-one years of age, she produced Cora II., dam of Dash II. who was whelped 1862. If any person desires to believe these things possible we have no objection, but we do object to any one thinking to overthrow the name of Laverack or disparage the great benefit he was to the breed because his pedigrees will not scan. What difference did it make if. Mr Laverack had simply stated that he had bred his setters from 1825, starting with a brace he had obtained from the Rev. A. Harrison, and interbred their progeny, that he had at various times tried outcrosses with reputable strains, but had never had satisfactory results and had come back to his old line again as closely as possible. The dogs would have been just as good individually, Countess would still have been the wonder she was, and there would have been no difference in the results of the Dan cross on the Laverack bitches, nor of the Laverack dogs on Dan's sisters. Mr. Laverack's setters were good because he had all the time been intent on their improvement, not because he gave with them a string of names in various order back to Old Moll and her consort Ponto.

It has been said that Mr. Laverack only bred to supply his own wants for shooting dogs, and then only when his brace in use were getting old did he rear a litter, pick out a new brace and repeat the operation. The known facts do not support this supposition, for he writes about many gentleman having his strain of setters, and from the amount of shooting he did he must have had a fairly well-filled kennel from which to draw his supply. Writing to his friend Rothwell, when he was an old man, November, 1874, he tells of having lost three puppies Rothwell had sent him, also six more and two brood bitches, eighteen months old, for which he had refused fifty guineas each, besides four more young dogs. Again in the first volume of the English stud book we find seven setters registered in his name, fifteen dogs bred by him registered as the property of others, and about twice as many

MR. PURCELL-LLEWELLYN'S COUNTESS
From Stonehenge's "Dogs of the British Islands"

MR. J. H. SHORTHOSE'S NOVEL
From "The Book of the Dog"

more bred from his dogs by other persons. It must also be understood that it never has been the custom to register dogs so freely in England as we do in this country, but it is left to the kennel club to enter free of charge all winners at field trials or at dog shows held under certain rules of the club. Hence Mr. Laverack's registered dogs were winners, and not one of his breeding stock was registered, as is the custom with us. Neither can we admit that his stud dogs were for the free use of every friend who wanted to breed to one of them. We do not say that he went into the business of breeding and selling to the extent that Mr. Llewellyn subsequently did, but there was no restriction of his operations merely for his own use. What improvement could a man possibly make by breeding a litter every six or seven years for fifty years? A breeder seeking to improve and build up a strain must have a surplus of stock for selection and only breed on from the best, so that we are forced to the conclusion that Mr. Laverack used a good many intermediate crosses not tabulated in his pedigrees, and felt his way along until he had his strain well established and universally acknowledged as of great merit.

Shortly after Mr. Laverack's book appeared, the talented editor of the London *Field*, the late Dr. J. H. Walsh, whose *nom de plume* of "Stonehenge" had world-wide fame, undertook a fourth edition of his "Dogs of the British Islands," and in this edition he personally wrote the sections on the setters, which were vast improvements on what appeared in prior editions written by contributors. This edition appeared in 1877 and covers the flush times of the Laveracks and the start of the "Llewellyns." Dr. Walsh knew greyhounds, setters and pointers better than he knew anything in the sporting world and, whenever he could, attended the field trials, and kept thoroughly in touch with what was going on. What he wrote is therefore "hot from the grid" compared with the fading recollections we have of what took place in England from 1876 to 1880. During the greater part of that period we contributed to the *Field*, knew Dr. Walsh personally and brought back to America an autograph letter accrediting us as his paper's representative at the New York dog show in 1880. This letter was immediately begged by Mr. Tileston, the Westminster Kennel Club's secretary, who, poor fellow, was killed the week prior to the date set for the show by the fall of the west wall of the old Madison Square Garden structure.

129

STONEHENGE ON LAVERACKS AND LLEWELLYNS

The opening paragraph of Stonehenge is as follows: "Since the publication of the articles on the various breeds of dogs in *The Field*, during the years 1856–57, the strain of setters known by the name of Laverack, from the gentleman who bred them, has carried all before it, both on the show bench and in the public field trials which have been held annually. For this high character it is greatly indebted to the celebrated Countess, who was certainly an extraordinary animal, both in appearance and at work; for, until she came out the only Laverack which had shone to advantage was Sir R. Garth's Daisy, a good average bitch. Though small, Countess was possessed of extraordinary pace, not perhaps equal to that of the still more celebrated pointer Drake, but approaching so closely to it that his superiority would be disputed by many of her admirers. Though on short legs, her frame is full of elegance, and her combined head and neck are absolutely perfect. With her high pace she combined great powers of endurance, and her chief fault was that she could never be fully depended upon; for when fresh enough to display her speed and style to the full, she would break away from her master and defy his whistle until she had taken her fling over a thousand acres or so. . . . On a good scenting day it was a great treat to see her at work, but, like most fast gallopers, she would sometimes flush her game on a bad scenting day, and then she would be wild with shame. Nellie (her sister) was of the same size, but not so fast, nor so elegant, still she was good enough to beat the crack on one occasion at Vaynol in 1872, but on most days she would have stood no chance with Countess. She served to show that Countess was not wholly exceptional, as was alleged by the detractors of the Laveracks; and these two bitches, together with Sir R. Garth's Daisy, may fairly be adduced as indicating that at all events the Laverack bitches are quite first class. No dog, however, has put in an appearance at any field trials with any pretension to high form, but several winners have appeared half or quarter bred of that strain."

Countess, although bred by Mr. Laverack, was run by Mr. Llewellyn, who bought her from Mr. Sam Lang, who got her from Mr. Laverack. Nellie was apparently bought direct from Mr. Laverack, as no mention is made of Mr. Lang in the stud book. Hence although she gave prominence to Mr. Llewellyn's kennel, the credit was really due to the Laverack strain. That all was not plain sailing for the Laveracks is apparent from this remark

CHAMPION CORA OF WETHERALL
Considered the most symmetrical setter of her sex during the time of her career

CINCINNATUS
Prominent on the bench a few years ago

131

of Stonehenge: "Before Daisy came out, Mr. Garth had produced a brace of very bad ones at Stafford, in 1867, and it was with considerable prejudice against them that the above celebrated bitches first exhibited their powers, in spite of the high character given them by Mr. Lort, Mr. Withington, and other well-known sportsmen who had shot over them for years. It is Mr. Lort's opinion that Mr. Withington possessed better dogs than even Countess, but it must not be forgotten that private trials are generally more flattering than those before the public." All of which goes to show that Stonehenge was a very conservative, unprejudiced writer, and what he says has added value on that account.

Stonehenge then proceeds to discuss what were the originals of what have come to be called "Llewellyns," and to show what this authority thought of the original title for these dogs we quote the opening paragraph: "I come now to consider the value of Mr. Llewellyn's 'field-trial' strain, as they are somewhat grandiloquently termed by their 'promoters,' or, as I shall call them, the 'Dan-Laveracks,' being all either by Dan out of Laverack bitches, or by a Laverack dog out of a sister to Dan."

If there were "promoters" in England, there were also promoters in this country, and they made it their business to give the most glowing accounts of the Llewellyns, late "field-trials" strain, so that not only were the American shooting public misled at that time, but nearly every person connected with field dogs since then has been, and is still, of the opinion that they were invincible in England from 1870 as long as Mr. Llewellyn continued to run dogs in the English field trials. Nothing could possibly be further from the truth, and while we could state the facts in our own way and be thoroughly accurate, yet any person who takes that position is still likely to be attacked as prejudiced or untruthful. In preference to that we will quote what Stonehenge wrote from his own knowledge and from the best information, publishing it when and where the facts were well known, that is, in England, and these statements were never called in question nor were his conclusions. Even there, however, the upholders of the Llewellyns were not as accurate in their statements as they should have been. One of them who wrote over the *nom de plume* of "Setter" is quoted by Stonehenge as saying: "During the past two years ten of the Laveracks and ten of the Duke-Rhoebe and Laverack cross have been sent to America: the former including Petrel, Pride of the Border, Fairy and Victress; the latter including Rock, Leicester, Rob Roy, Dart and Dora, the same men being owners of both sorts. At the American shows both sorts have appeared, and the Rhoebe blood has always beaten the Laverack. At field trials no Laverack has been entered, but first, second and third prizes were gained at their last field trials, in the champion stakes, by dogs of the Rhoebe blood, all descended from Mr. Llewellyn's kennels." In the first place, the same men did not own the setters named, Mr. L. H. Smith, of Strathroy, Ont., being the only one to possess representatives of each lot. As to the wins, the first champion stakes of record, run in 1876, had Drake, Stafford and Paris placed in that order. Drake was bred by Mr. Luther Adams and was by the Laverack dog Prince, out of Dora, who was bred by Mr. Statter and was by Duke out of Rhoebe. A very strange record of breeding to claim to have come from Mr. Llewellyn's kennels. Stonehenge very pertinently remarks that as the two strains had not met afield there was no indication of superiority, and that without any definite knowledge he was quite prepared to admit superiority on the bench, as the Laverack dogs were heavy and lumbering, and the bitches, "though very elegant, too small and delicate for perfection."

Going on to discuss merits of the field trials performers as shown in England, Stonehenge says: "Now, although I have always regarded Duke himself as on the whole a good dog, especially in pace and range, and have estimated Dan and Dick, the result of his cross with Mr. Statter's Rhoebe, favourably, as compared with the Laverack litters as shown in Bruce and Rob Roy, yet I never considered Dan as a good cross for the Laverack bitches, because his sire always showed a want of nose similar to the Laveracks themselves. Duke is said by 'Setter,' and I believe correctly, to have received a high character from Mr. Barclay Field for his nose as exhibited in private, but he was notoriously deficient in this quality when brought before the public, going with his head low and feeling the foot rather than the body scent. In proof of this defect it is only necessary to say that he was beaten by Hamlet and Young Kent in this quality at Bala, in 1867, when the judge gave him only thirty-one out of a possible forty for nose, while at Stafford in the following spring Rex found birds twenty yards behind the place where he had left his point, thereby gaining the cup, Sir V. Corbett, the breeder of Duke, being one of the judges and loud in his admiration of Rex's nose, while finding fault with that of Duke. Indeed, this defect was always made the excuse for E. Armstrong's constant interference with him by hand and voice—whether rightly or wrongly

I do not pretend to say, but it evidently marked that clever breaker's want of confidence in his dog's nose. Of Rhoebe herself I do not recollect enough to give an opinion as to this quality in her individually, and among her produce I do not remember any but Bruce and Dan that displayed even an average amount of scenting powers. Rob Roy was notoriously deficient in nose; and Dick, brother to Dan, in his second season was constantly making false points, and is so described in the report of the Southampton Trials of 1872. For these reasons, although I had always considered the Duke-Rhoebe cross superior to the two Laverack-Rhoebe litters, I never expected Dan to get such a good bitch as Norna, in point of nose and correct carriage of head and flag, according to my ideas. If Nora, as alleged by her owner and 'Setter,' as well as by the *Field* reporter at Horseheath, is superior to her, I can only make my apology to Dan and admit that he has turned out a better sire than I expected, and than might have been gathered from the performances of Laura, Leda, and Druid, at the Devon and Cornwall, and Sleaford trials of 1874, which I saw.

"Taking into consideration that the dogs which have been exhibited by Mr. Llewellyn have been picked from a very large kennel, and that as far as I have seen them perform, they have not proved themselves to be above the average, I can only come to the conclusion that Dan has not done any great good in improving the Laveracks, except in looks and size. Neither do I place him or any of his stock in the first rank of field trials winners, which in setters would I think include only Countess, Ranger, and Dash II., forming with the pointers Drake and Belle, a quintet in class A1. Dan came out in public only once it is true, though winning three stakes at that meeting, but he met the same dogs in all, and the victory was virtually only a single one. After this he put his shoulder out and never appeared in public again, but his brother Dick, who was coupled in 🔲 braces with him, and went equally well in the short trial accorded them, did not do anything worth speaking of next year. . . . Moreover Dan had at Shrewsbury a very narrow escape of defeat by Rake, as recorded by myself at the time, so that on mature reflection I have no hesitation in placing him below the first class, but possibly he is entitled to rank in the second class along with Plunket and his son and daughter, Kite and Music, (Irish), together with Kate, Rex and Lang (Gordons). To them may be probably added the Dan-Laveracks Norna and Nora and also Die, all more or less crossed with the late Mr. Laverack's strain. To sum up, therefore, it may be safely alleged that his (Laverack's) setters have been of great service to sportsmen in giving pace and style when crossed with other breeds."

Those entitled by experience to enter into any controversy on the subject of Mr. Laverack's and Mr. Llewellyn's setters know only too well that the authority thus quoted cannot be gainsaid in any facts, and that the arguments with which he leads up to his opinions are exceedingly hard to controvert. That then was the position of the Llewellyns in England at the very time they were being forced upon the American market by a very much interested coterie intent on striking the financial iron while they were keeping it hot.

Even in Shaw's "Book of the Dog," published in 1880, there is no intimation that Mr. Llewellyn had "set the Thames on fire" with his world beaters, and the only references to that gentleman are: "Mr. R. Ll. Purcell-Llewellyn is one of our greatest Laverack breeders of the day, and spares no trouble or expense in perfecting his strain. . . . Count Wind'em, Countess Bear and Countess Moll are the bright particular stars of Mr. Llewellyn's kennel, and the first named is a great, big, useful-looking dog." We do not advance the latter quotations as in any way conclusive, for it is very evident that the setter article in that book was a piece of patch work, written by various persons, but that there is no mention of what was at that time to Americans the most wonderful combination of ability and good looks proves that they were exciting very little attention in England compared with what the agitation in the American press had accomplished in this country.

Early Importations of Laveracks

The success of the Laveracks in England, coupled with the interest engendered here by the publication of Mr. Laverack's book, unavoidably inspired American progressive sportsmen with the wish to secure some of the much-to-be-desired breed, and when it was announced early in 1874 that Mr. Laverack was offering for sale a brace of his dogs, he became the recipient of many inquiries, and of several offers to purchase them. Upon receipt of a communication accompanied by a draft for the amount asked, he shipped to New York the first pair of his dogs exported to this country, where they arrived in July of that year. These dogs were Pride of the Border, and Fairy, purchased by Mr. Charles H. Raymond, of Fox

CHAMPION COUNT RENO
A Pacific Coast son of Albert's Fleet

MR. R. H. BARRY'S MYRTLE BEATRICE

Farm, Morris Plains, N. J., Fairy coming over in whelp to Laverack's Blue Prince, a son of Pride of the Border.

In appearance the imported pair did not greatly resemble each other. Pride of the Border, although not a large dog, was somewhat heavily made, with long, low action, and liver and white in colour. Fairy, although stoutly built, was smaller, of lighter frame and quicker in movement, and was an orange Belton. Both were wide rangers, and possessed extraordinary powers of scent. In this latter particular Pride of the Border was a remarkable dog. At first he was apparently indifferent to or puzzled by the scent of our game birds, but when he became acclimated and grew accustomed to the new conditions, he developed into a most satisfactory shooting dog. When in the field his intelligence seemed always actively at work, and in getting to his birds his head saved his heels many an unnecessary rod's travel. Like one of the blue Beltons described by Mr. Laverack, this dog displayed wonderful sagacity on running birds; for instance, pointing an old cock grouse, or a running brood, he knew by the scent when the game had left him; then, instead of footing, immediately sunk or dropped down wind thirty or forty yards and re-pointed, his sagacity telling him he could find game much quicker by taking advantage of the wind than 'footing.' When working on quail or ruffed grouse, Pride of the Border constantly resorted to these tactics whenever the birds 'roaded.' When on his game he 'set' instead of pointing; lying down with neck extended like a dog at 'down charge,' reminding one of Laverack's expressed belief that 'most breeders of any note agree that the setter is nothing more than the setting spaniel improved.'"

Pride and Fairy showed to great advantage on the open snipe meadow, ranging widely and pointing and backing staunchly, and they would doubtless have made an equally effective brace on wide prairies. Fairy was faster than the dog, and more animated in her work, but like him was round ribbed and deep chested. Both were thorough "gun dogs," caring little for anything save seeking and finding game. They were never run in field trials—then in their infancy here—being reserved by their owner for his personal use in the field. Pride was never publicly advertised in the stud, but was bred to several bitches from various parts of the country, and some of his progeny were later imported by other fanciers. In 1881 we compiled a record of the get of Pride of the Border which showed that of the fifty-six Laveracks then in this country, forty-six were descendants of this

137

noted dog. As quite a number of setter breeders of the present time are often at a loss to decide whether certain old dogs were or were not pure bred Laveracks, we give this record of 1881, exactly as we published it two years later in the old American Kennel Register.

Pride of the Border's Progeny—First Generation

Out of Fairy: Charm, Guy Mannering, Roderick Dhu, Brough, Ranger.

Out of Petrel: Shafto, Pontiac, Pride, Petrel II., Princess Nellie.

Out of Fairy II.: Thunder, Duke of Beaufort.

Out of Ruby: Diamond, Daisy Dean.

SECOND GENERATION

From Carlowitz (imported), out of Princess Nellie: True Blue, Carlina, Lilly, Sting II., Count Noser, Carmot.

From Blue Prince, out of Fairy: Young Laverack (imported).

From Pontiac, out of Fairy: Fate, Etoile.

From Pontiac, out of Fairy II: Fairy Prince, Lance, Laverack Chief, Fairy III.

From Thunder, out of Peeress: Dick Laverack, Prince Laverack, Mack Laverick, Maple, Coomassie, Lady Laverack, Daisy Laverack, Pet Laverack, Lu Laverack, Peggy Laverack.

From Young Laverack, out of Petrel II.: Lora Laverack.

From Carlowitz, out of Daisy Dean: Bonny Kate, Sir Hal, Leo X.

To this second generation there was added two years later the dog Emperor Fred, sent over and first shown here in the name of Mr. Robinson, but afterward as the property of E. A. Herzberg, of Brooklyn, who returned as part payment to Mr. Robinson the dog Aldershot, a son of Emperor Fred, whose name appears in the third generation which we now give.

THIRD GENERATION

From Tam O'Shanter, out of La Reine: Blue Queen and Don Juan both imported.

MR. FRANK G. TAYLOR'S CHAMPION KNIGHT ERRANT
A widely shown dog from 1898 to 1900

DR. J. E. HAIR'S CHAMPION HIGHLAND FLEET

From Bailey's Victor, out of Blue Daisy: Fairy II. and Magnet. These were credited in the stud book to Mr. Laverack as breeder, but we satisfied ourselves at the time that they were bred by Mr. Robinson, of Sunderland, who was the canine legatee of Mr. Laverack.

From Emperor Fred, out of Blue Cora: Aldershot.

All three of these dams were by Blue Prince, son of Pride of the Border, and Emperor Fred was also by Blue Prince.

The foregoing were of course not all of the get of Pride of the Border, for it was only the living descendants at that time that were tabulated, and Pride had also been bred to other than pure Laverack bitches, getting that excellent show and field dog St. Elmo out of a short pedigreed bitch of Herzberg's.

In speaking to Mr. Raymond recently about the old dog and his descendants he told us that he still had some setters that traced to him, and whenever trained they were found to be excellent field dogs. Those were not pure Laveracks, however; indeed, we believe it would be impossible to find one anywhere that had such a claim. As to the controversies which have taken place regarding Laverack pedigrees, Mr. Raymond never in any way took part, he being thoroughly satisfied with the high character and excellence of the dogs themselves, without discussing old, unnecessary subjects, which had no bearing on the individuality of the dogs.

Other importations followed Mr. Raymond's and for ten years the Laveracks had their full share of success on the show bench. The series of importations of this strain terminating with that of Emperor Fred, a remarkably good dog that never really got his deserts in this country. He was first shown at New York in 1881, and led in th· class for imported setter dogs. The term "imported" including the progeny of imported dogs, so that Duke of Beaufort and Pontiac, both by Pride of the Border, the former out of Fairy II., and the latter out of Petrel, though bred here, were in this class, and these three Laveracks were placed in the order named. When it came to the breed special, Thunder, another Laverack, beat Emperor Fred, though the latter was an immeasurably superior dog. Thunder was a big winner at that period, but very faulty in essential points, though quite a taking dog to the non-expert. The judge on this occasion was not the only one to make this blunder, but as sound judges were not by any means plentiful at that time, awards by the non-experts must be accepted with caution. Emperor Fred finally had justice done him at Washington in 1883, when Mr. Mason placed him first in a wonderfully strong class of champions —dogs which had won first in the open class. Here he defeated Thunder, Don Juan, Plantagenet, Coin, and Foreman. So successful were the Laveracks up to that time that at this show the classification for English setters was divided into sections for Laveracks of pure breeding and "except pure Laveracks." But this was almost the end of this short-lived division, for the glamour of the field-trial performances of certain dogs twisted the setter-judging to such an extent that Laveracks became practically extinct.

With the departure of Emperor Fred from the ring, Plantagenet was about the best setter of 1884. Foreman, it is true, defeated him, but while there was room for difference of opinion, we always favoured the more quality-looking Plantagenet, for Foreman was a very heavy-headed dog. short and round in skull and rather short bodied, "chucked up," in fact, Nevertheless he was a very impressive dog, a good, vigorous mover, with superb hindquarters, and but for a slight turning out of the forefeet, and not being quite straight enough in pasterns to please the fastidious, he was a dog of grand character, and this, coupled with his superb coat, both in quantity and quality, made him a setter that should have pleased both sections of the fancy. It soon became noised abroad that he was a good field dog, so that when he won the champion stakes at the Eastern Field Trials Club meeting he sprang into deserved popularity as a sire with beneficial results, more particularly in getting bitches of quality, such as Haphazard, Calico, Saddlebags, Daisy Foreman and others, all decided acquisitions on the score of shape and appearance, though all showing more or less the roundness of skull and shortness of muzzle, with the pinched appearance their sire displayed. We take it, however, that he was the next dog to do good to the setter following Pride of the Border.

The Era of Mr. Windholz and the Blackstone Kennels

We now come to an era that warms the heart of those who can recall the dogs of 1885 and following years during which the dogs of Mr. Windholz played such a conspicuous part at the leading shows of that period. This gentleman started his prominent show career with Rockingham and Princess Beatrice, and, as the former remained an unbeaten dog for some time, it is always with considerable personal satisfaction we recall the facts attending

BARTON TORY

A prominent dog in the present-day revival of the correct type of English setters, which began four years ago

STYLISH SERGEANT

A leading show dog in England and America, now at Seattle, Washington

142

his purchase. We visited England in the early winter of 1884, and the only show of importance we had an opportunity of seeing was that at Hull. There we met our old friend Billy Graham, from Belfast, who, by the way, took the special for best four of any breed with the best matched team of Irish terriers we have ever seen benched by any person. Mr. Graham told us he had an order for a brace of setters for Mr. Windholz and wanted our opinion on a dog that was at the show. We had already had a casual glance along the benches and had noted a very likely looking dog and, remembering his whereabouts, we located the dog when Mr. Graham was trying to do so. It was the dog we had noticed. He was in very poor condition, thin as a rail and looking wretched. We took him down and in reply to the question as to whether he could be got right, Mr. Graham said he was positive he could, as he had seen him in good shape and his condition then was the result of sickness. "Then buy him if you are sure of that, for if he can be got right he will beat any setter we have," was our advice. So Graham bought the dog and later secured an excellent mate for him in Princess Phœbus. Rockingham was one of those dogs fitly described by one of the critics of that day who, when not exactly sure of his ground, summed up a dog as having no glaring faults—slightly strong in head, but of good type and excellent expression and needing a little more bend to the hocks and a little less flatness of back. A few changes of that sort would have been very great improvements in a dog that even without them was an excellent type all over, and with his lovely coat was one that gave pleasure to look at. He was a good dog to shoot over, and so were his get, Mr. Windholz always taking a fall shooting trip to the South in those days.

Unfortunately, neither this good dog nor his sire Belthus, then in this country, were bred to to any extent, nor as men of intelligence in the breed should have done. Breeders went after strange gods in those days with results we shall soon have to touch upon. Mr. Windholz followed up these importations with those of Count Howard, Cora of Wetherall, Countess Zoe and Princess Beatrice, and could show a team the counterpart of which we never saw until Mr. Vandergrift took up the breed a few years ago. The rival to Mr. Windholz was the Blackstone Kennels of Pawtucket, and as Foreman could not defeat Rockingham, Mr. Crawford decided to import one that might do so. The result was the oncoming of Royal Albert, who finally succeeded in winning from the older dog at New York in 1887. The question was not by any means considered settled thereby, for the con-

sensus of opinion was that the setters at this show were very badly judged.
We might add to that that we *know* they were not properly judged, but as
the awarder of the ribbons has joined the majority, this is neither the time
nor the place to speak further. Another excellent importation was Royal
Prince II., shown most successfully through the shows of 1887 and 1889.

The Dark Days of the "Tennessee Setters"

A very good American-bred dog was competing at this time named
Roger, getting either first or second at a number of good shows. He was
shown for three years at New York, and was second on each occasion. He
was a big, sound dog, of good conformation, but failed in quality just
enough to keep him out of the top rank. One would imagine that with all
this education as to what an English setter should look like it would have
been impossible for any person qualified to judge the breed to go wrong, but
such was not the case. Judges who had seen dogs at the field trials did not
seem able to forget that the sires of certain dogs shown under them in the
ring had run well in the field, and it must have been on that account alone
that many decisions were made by men who had placed dogs properly on
prior occasions and have shown better judgment since then.

As most of these singular and angular dogs came from Tennessee, those
who attacked the bad judging gave them the name of the "Tennessee
setters" and derided them to the full extent of their ability. Occasionally
since then we have been asked what a Tennessee setter is, the inquirer being
under the impression that it was some specially good line of the breed. As
illustrative of what the "Tennessee setters" looked like we give the criticism
of Mr. Mason on the dog that won first and special in a class of twenty-four
dogs at a leading show of 1887, the extract being from "Our Prize Dogs"—
a most valuable contribution to kennel literature, containing full descrip-
tions with criticism on all the prize winners of that period:

"Skull and muzzle fairly good, also eyes, ears and lips. Neck well
formed and of sufficient length. Chest very defective, the ribs showing
scarcely any deviation from a straight line, and being attached to the vertebræ in about the same way that the legs of a milking stool are set in. The
result of this structural defect is a narrow, slab-sided chest, lacking incapacity
for lodgment of heart and lungs, and a narrow, weak back. The short ribs
should be much deeper and better spread, and the loin, instead of being flat,

144

MR. A. ALBRIGHT, JR.'S QUEEN'S PLACE PRIDE
Photo by Schreibe
One of the many good setters imported by Mr. J. B. Vandergrift

G. C. THOMAS, JR.'S ULVERSTONE RAP
Photo by Schreiber
An imported dog and consistent winner

145

narrow and tucked up, should show strength, not only in width but in depth. The vertebræ instead of protruding so as to leave a line down the back like the edge of a saw, should be well clothed on both sides with hard muscle. Quarters very light, and showing defects such as we have never seen overlooked by a judge of the breed. Thighs resembling those of a cat, being narrow and flat, and from a back view showing none of the beautiful lines which always portray speed and power, and which are indispensable in dogs which must go and stay. Hocks straight and light; they should be well bent, strong and clean. Forelegs not quite straight. Shoulders moderate. Feet fairly good. Tail long and curled over the back. Stands low at the shoulder in proportion to height at quarters. A small, weedy-looking dog, having body and limbs for which there is no standard and probably never will be."

The second to this dog was summarised as follows: "An undersized, slab-sided, light-quartered, ring-tailed and bad-headed specimen, having few if any show points. After having examined very carefully this and other dogs at this show, we can readily understand why a new standard was contemplated."

The cause of this perversion of the English setter type is to be traced to the introduction of the Llewellyns, not that the imported dogs were such weeds, but that the incompetence of breeders and the complete ignoring of anything like advisability in breeding let loose a flood of wretchedly built dogs, and judges who had knowledge of field trials did not seem able to properly place dogs descended from racing progenitors competing with true-built dogs of type, when it came to judging points in the show ring. With them the fact that a dog was descended from parents of excellent field qualifications was evidently ample reason for placing that dog high in the prize list. Their judging was very much on the order of the old gamekeeper's who, having been persuaded to don the ermine, took a glance over the candidates till his eye lighted on one that made him at once decide the placing by saying, "That looks like our old Bill, give him first."

What these "Llewellyns" were has never been lucidly determined, and later-day writers and supporters of the title acknowledge that no rule can be framed to interpret the name clearly. We all know what a Laverack was— a dog from Mr. Laverack's kennels, or descended from such, without any outside blood; but Mr. Llewellyn had no strain at all in his kennel. He had dabbled in Irish setters, bought "cracks" of full Laverack blood, such as

Countess and her sister, and then some more winners of Mr. Statter's breeding. These he crossed, not as anything new or patented by him, but merely what many other English breeders were then doing. He, however, had the very good fortune to sell some of his dogs to some Americans, who at once proceeded to exploit the "strain," and, to differentiate them from the Laveracks, styled them Llewellyns. Now we have dogs from that breeder's kennels which were not of the cross between the Statter setters and the Laveracks, for Mr. Llewellyn very soon introduced different blood; and on the other hand, we have had dogs of this Dan-Laverack strain, as Stonehenge called the cross, which Mr. Llewellyn never saw. That Llewellyn enthusiast, Mr. Joseph A. Graham, of St. Louis, in "The Sporting Dog," frankly and honestly says that it is impossible to give a definition that will hold good. He says the exclusionists' definition of Duke-Rhoebe and Laverack will not hold good because it shuts out "a large number of the most respected names in Llewellyn pedigrees;" meaning dogs bought from that breeder with later crosses of Dash II. blood. Then he says that to limit the title to dogs which had come from Mr. Llewellyn's kennel would exclude all the Blue Beltons and several others. These exclusionists wanted to keep out the Gleam strain because of his descent from another outside cross, that of Sam; but now they have let down the bars and the Gleams are in the inner circle. Finally, Mr. Graham says it "would be as well to go further and drop the 'pure' idea altogether, letting Llewellyn blood stand for what it is—an influential but not separate element in English setter breeding." But he still leaves us puzzling as to what this Llewellyn blood is. Is it everything that Mr. Llwellyn bred from all sorts of outside sources, and everything that others bred at the same time and in the same way as he did, or what?

Bringing this question down to the present times, there was a special offered by Mr. Graham at the St. Louis Exposition dog show for the best Llewellyn dog and another for the best Llewellyn bitch. When it came to the judging Ben Lewis took in his regular class winners, Bracken o'Leck and Lansdowne Mallwyd Di. There was much discussion in the ring as to eligibility, and Mr. Marsh Byers, the judge, finally said as no one could give any definition or show any published condition governing the special, he could only judge the dogs claimed to be Llewellyns and the class awards were followed. We later saw the official judges' record and there was a memorandum "disqualified" against these winners, but by whom made

147

or for what reason we were unable to find out. Mr. Lewis told us that some of the dog's ancestors had come from Mr. Llewellyn's kennels, and if that is so then Mr. Graham's own book could be cited in support of the eligibility of these two dogs.

Be it understood that we have no objection to the naming, in some special way, of a branch of the setter family bred for the particular purpose of running in field trials, but we do hold that no person can purchase a bitch from one man and a dog from another and in four months the progeny of this brace are eligible to be given his name as a distinguishing title, which is just what the so-called Llewellyns amount to.

We have already referred to the manner in which they were forced to the front in dog shows, by placing crudely shaped animals, bred from dogs with field trial records, over much better setters; but it is not to be denied that the same methods were adopted in field trials, until it was almost a matter of necessity to run dogs of certain breeding to win at these contests. There is far greater latitude in field trials for the exercise of individual opinion—what Mr. John Davidson has aptly styled the judge's "think"— than in dog shows, and this was exercised to the full in field trials. By these means all opposition was swamped and the result was most conspicuous in the shrunken classes of setters at the shows of the period which followed the bad work we have referred to. Not only that, but type was cast to the winds, and only at intervals were dogs of the right sort placed where they ought to be. It was, indeed, dark days for the English setter for about five years beginning about 1887.

As Mr. Mason hinted in his criticisms quoted above, new standards were made to fit the new dogs; but those who held to the old cult would have none of the new idea, and the first fell flat, as has also the second; and so radically wrong was the latest "made-to-fit standard" that it resulted in the formation of an English setter club which adopted a standard more in keeping with what an English setter really is.

That this field trials strain of setters did good, we do not for a moment question. Greater interest was developed in the breeding and running of dogs at the trials, which also increased rapidly in number and importance; but any claim that our excellent class of field trials dogs is due entirely to being able to trace back through several generations to two or three dogs, is not tenable for a moment. In an article published recently in *Country Life in America*, we stated our opinion that if there had been no importations to speak of, the same amount of work in breeding to notable performers, a similar number of their progeny to select the young entry from and the same amount of labour expended in their training would have made just as high a grade as we have now. If it was all in the blood, in this particular Dan-Laverack cross, why was it that Mr. Llewellyn had to go outside for new blood, and then drop down to the bottom again with his field trials entries.

It was little wonder that with bad dogs put in front breeders were all at sea in knowing what to breed to for type. Dogs went up and down in the prize lists—H. C. at some second-class show and second at New York, then back again to a commendation. The result was that every breeder could find warrant in breeding to almost any kind of a built dog, and most of them bred to dogs that had won in the field, no matter what they looked like. The natural result followed of worse mixed classes than we had had at any time since the introduction of the Laveracks and the separation of imported dogs from natives, a distinction that had long been done away with.

It was not until about 1892 that we began to see daylight again, and although Albert's Ranger, imported at that time, was lacking in some of the essentials we deem necessary in a field dog, he was yet a dog of exceptional quality, and in some respects of type also. Almost at the same time Cincinnatus Pride appeared, a dog lacking in quality compared with those of the best type, but still of good parts and symmetry. For several years these two held sway in the show ring till Sheldon came out. This was a remarkably good son of Rockingham, and it was undoubtedly a most unfortunate thing that hardly had this grand dog been discovered than he was lost to breeders. Coming out at New York in 1896, he defeated both the dogs just named, and although the decision was much discussed, it was upheld at the four succeeding shows under different judges, one being a very severe critic of the first award. For seven shows he kept up his winning gait and then fell sick and died. He was a dog of grand formation and all a setter, while he was of great quality. Those opposed to his successes kept calling him a Laverack, possibly under the impression that that was a term of reproach, forgetting that his dam was by Belton, a Duke-Rhœbe-Laverack bred one, and eligible to the inner circles of exclusiveness; although, lamentably for the sake of the name Llewellyn, Mr. Statter bred Belton before Mr. Llewellyn ever owned Dan, with which he is claimed to have started the line of dogs given his name as originator. Sheldon's

CHARITY

COUNT OAKLEY

JOE CUMMING

DOC HICK

RODFIELD

A great fielddrials performer

record shows him to have been very decidedly the best American-bred dog of that date, if not up to that time.

Sheldon would probably never have been shown if he had not been "discovered" by that good judge of a setter and experienced breeder, Dr. J. E. Hair, of Bridgeport, Conn. Up to that time he had been kept as a private shooting dog, with no knowledge of how good he was from a show point of view. Had he lived we are fully of the opinion that he would have done wonders for the setter, for from the few bitches he was bred to each of his get was a winner, and the second generation are to-day about the only American-bred setters that have reached the title of champion during the past two or three years.

A setter which had a great reputation in the West now made his appearance in the East, Rodfield, and although he was anything but a good dog, he eventually got his champion title through winning three firsts in the open class under fanciers of the field trials bred dogs, and then with no opposition in the challenge class at small Western shows he got the necessary three wins, a process which could not be repeated under present conditions. A far better dog was Cincinnatus Pride, for Rodfield was short in head and thick in skull, full in eyes, with an exceedingly bad front and weak pasterns to offset his good neck, body and quarters. Because he was a field trials winner he was bred to extensively, but as any person with knowledge of the rudiments of breeding could have foretold, he got worse-looking progeny than he was himself. Cincinnatus Pride was not a good-headed dog, but nevertheless close to the best in those bad days for the breed. Still the judges of that time would not have him till one day he did well at a field trials; whereupon, although he could not be as good a dog as when younger, he at once jumped from third and V.H.C. to first place and went over dogs that should have beaten him. He was then bred to very extensively, and it is gratifying to say that he materially improved the field trials dogs, it being to that class of bitches he was mostly bred. It does not appear, however, that he produced anything equal to himself in general merit for show purposes. It is not so very certain that those who breed for type did not miss an opportunity when they overlooked this dog, for on his dam's side he was wonderfully well bred, the lines running quickly to such excellent setters as Rock, Rum, Sir Allister, Belton, Fletcher's Rock, Novel and other well-known setters of the past, and if used to good-quality bitches he might have been a success.

151

The end of the mixed-up condition of affairs seemed to be about 1898, or rather that was about the beginning of the much-to-be-desired change to something more stable. Albert's Woodcock came over that year and won through to winners' class at New York, followed by a dog of much similar type. These were English setters, dogs of substance, typical and showing character. Neither was a wonder, but they were nearer to the right sort than we had seen since Sheldon's day. Quite a nice American-bred dog was also shown in Highland Fleet, though as he was from imported stock he would under the old-time rule have still been considered as imported, as opposed to native. Fleet suffered from being somewhat under the desired size, but showing much quality and was well put together. He did not do very well at his first show, but attracted the eye of Doctor Hair, so soon found another owner. His name was not changed to the "Albert" prefix and he is known on the records as Highland Fleet, with the addition of "champion." Like the unfortunate Sheldon, he did not live long at the Bridgeport kennels, being poisoned the following year, but not before he left some nice descendants, some of which were winners, and two championship winners of 1904 are but two removes from him.

Knight Errant was also a very prominent dog in 1900, though not one we altogether fancied, and when it came to placing him over Barton Tory at New York the following year we do think the judge made a mistake. Barton Tory was not a perfect dog, especially in hind legs, but his quality put him in a higher class than anything we then had.

With the new century came flush times for the right sort of setters. Mr. Vandergrift took hold of the breed with the thoroughness that had characterised his connection with bulldogs and soon had a splended collection of bitches and several good dogs, besides Barton Tory. The latter, while a very good dog, as already stated, was frequently rated too high in competition for specials against the best of other breeds. At Providence he erroneously won a cup for the best in the show. His poor hindquarters were then all too conspicuous and there were several far more perfect dogs in the ring. We were one of a party of six judges on that occasion and our vote was for the mastiff Prince of Wales, the others voting for the setter or a toy spaniel. The mastiff eventually got the reserve. The setter was then mated with a far better bitch, and the toy spaniel in the

LORD BENTINCK, TAKEN WHEN SEVEN YEARS OLD
One of the famous sires of recent days in England

MR. F. SHUNK BROWN'S ENGLISH SETTER EDGEMARK
A prominent winner a few years ago

153

previous class was mated with a poorer one. The majority having decided that Barton Tory was the best dog in the show, we of course voted for him and his better mate, only to find ourselves once more in the minority, the defeated toy and his inferior mate getting the most votes. Several similar experiences followed, and we have ever since eschewed judging specials in mixed company.

The gems of Mr. Vandergrift's kennel were in the excellent collection of bitches, including Queen's Place Pride, Queen's Pride, Queen's Flora and one or two others. At the same time it was not all plain sailing for even this good kennel for Mr. G. C. Thomas, Jr., of Philadelphia, was also in the ring with his Bloomfield kennels, which shortly included Mallwyd Sirdar, Stylish Sergeant, Dido B., Mepal's Queen B., Pera, and others. Mr. Thomas was the better stayer of the two exhibitors, the Vancroft kennels being given up the following year. It looked lately as if Mr. Thomas was also preparing to go on the retired list, but fortunately it is not so, for at the close of 1904 he purchased from Ben Lewis his entire kennel of English setters and the latter will keep out of the breed, only showing for Mr. Thomas for a year from the date of sale.

Mr. Barry, of Rye, is another of the standard sort, holding to his own course in storm and sunshine, keeping good setters to look at and good to shoot over, and breeding a little on lines that promise well, but no one will gainsay that the stick-fast-to-type is Doctor Hair, and too much credit cannot be given him by all who value the perpetuation of an old breed in its purity of type for his consistent course for so many years.

At no time since the early eighties has prospects for the English setter looked more favorable than at present. Show committees are giving exhibitors better judges, and whatever fear there was of offending field trials men has been overcome. Even if we do occasionally have a judge who speaks of two types and thinks it right to put one of each in the prize list, he does not do it to any extent. If a man will not judge to one type, the type he believes to be correct, he has no business in the ring, for he is obliging some exhibitors at the expense of others and against what should be his immovable opinion and verdict.

Pedigree in Field Trials Dogs

There seems to be far more misconception as to which line of blood we are more particularly indebted to for the excellence of the dogs bred for field sports and with a view of possibly approaching field trials form, than any person not conversant with the facts could imagine possible. It has become so much a matter of custom to accept the dictum that we owe everything to the original importations from Mr. Llewellyn's kennels and other dogs of similar breeding, that it is generally believed that Gladstone is the main reliance in pedigrees and that all modern field trials performers are of his family.

We cannot make any change in the arranging of families in dogs from what is the custom in grouping other animals, and therefore take the male line as authoritative. We are indebted to Major J. M. Taylor for a vast amount of unrequited labour in getting up his book of "Bench Show and Field Trials Records," which covers the ground up to the close of 1891, valuable statistical information being included with the plain records. Here we find, from a thorough supporter of the Gladstone family, a table of the successful get of that dog, also what Count Noble accomplished and every other sire of a field trials winner or placed dog. Gladstone, Count Noble and Roderigo are however taken out of the alphabetical sequence as being dogs of prominence as sires. Gladstone up to the close of 1891—he was born in 1876 and died in 1890—had sired twenty-five dogs, which had obtained a place in the trials. Count Noble, imported 1880, died 1891, is credited with twenty-eight sons and daughters, and we may say that the tables show the two families as tied for honours, as each had fourteen firsts and nineteen thirds to its credit, the only difference being that Gladstone led by two points on second place and Count Noble by three as to fourth place. That, however, is the only point where there is an equality.

If we had had to rely upon the male descendants in that Gladstone record for the carrying on of the family honours it would have been a broken reed, for with the exception of Paul Gladstone not one became famous, and he to a limited extent only. On the other hand, Count Noble sired such remarkable performers and sires as Gath, Roderigo, Cincinnatus, and Count Gladstone IV. It is quite true that Gladstone bitches had much to do with the success of Count Noble, and that it was probably the latter's good fortune in that respect that led to his very great success. Had the tables been turned and Gladstone followed Count Noble, the result might have been satisfactory to the admirers of the latter family, but we cannot deal with probabilities and must take the records as we find them.

Gath, who died young, left a few very good dogs to carry on his line.

He was out of a Gladstone bitch and when bred back to the Gladstone bitch Gem threw the litter in which were Gath's Mark and Gath's Hope. This line has not been so successful of late as have others, however. Roderigo was a most successful son of Count Noble. He also was out of a Gladstone bitch, and we have from him a number of lines, prominent among them being Antonio, from whom we had Rodfield, Tony Boy and Tony Gale, and there is little prospect at present of losing tracings to Antonio and Roderigo in the best dogs at the field trials. Count Gladstone IV. is bred like Roderigo, and he was another most successful sire, his son, Lady's Count Gladstone, being the phenomenal sire of 1904 in field trial records, no less than fourteen placed dogs being by him, while second to him come Count Danstone, his litter brother, and Rodfield, each with four to his credit during the year.

While Count Noble was purely Dan-Laverack, he had an extra infusion of Laverack blood through his sire Count Wind'em, who was by the Dan-Laverack dog Count Dick, out of the pure Laverack Phantom, a sister to Petrel, dam of Gladstone. This makes the Count Noble and Gladstone cross very close in-breeding, for in the pedigree of Count Noble we have Count Dick, already mentioned, by Dan out of Countess, and Nora, the dam, was by Dan out of Nellie, sister to Countess. Then Phantom and Peeress the other two bitches in the pedigree are, as already stated, full sisters.

Again we have the dam of Lady's Count Gladstone and Count Danstone, in-bred also. This was Dan's Lady, by Dan Gladstone, son of Gladstone out of the Druid bitch Sue; and Lady's dam by Gath's Mark, by Gath out of Gem, both with a Gladstone cross. In Dan's Lady we have a cross of Dash III., a dog that is not Llewellyn according to any reasonable interpretation of what that word may mean. He was bred by John Armstrong, and was by a Laverack dog out of Old Kate, who was by another Laverack out of the pedigreeless E. Armstrong's Kate. Dash III. became quite prominent in pedigrees of noted performers, and it behooved the promoters of the "Llewellyns" to do something to keep the winners within their fold, so they decided to extend the pale and admit the pedigreeless Kate as worthy of becoming a progenitor of the commercial breed. This was no novelty for a similar thing was done in the case of Dash II. and Sam, dogs introduced into Mr. Llewellyn's kennels as out-crosses; something he was always practising, and as soon as it became evident that breeders were climbing over the fence and breeding outside of the already proscribed limits, the promoters met the emergency by extending the limits and so keep all the good dogs as "Llewellyns."

To our mind the excellence of the American field dog is owing to the concentration of effort in the securing a dog to suit the special requirements in our field trials. Breeders have bred to the winning dogs and kept on at that, and while there have been thousands bred annually not worth feeding, yet out of the great number there were bound to be some good ones.

DOCTOR ROWE ON THE LLEWELLYNS

Many readers who have accepted the statements of persons no better informed than themselves regarding the Llewellyns may perhaps be of the opinion that we are either incorrect or prejudiced in what we have previously stated in the article in *Country Life in America*, already mentioned, and also herein. We propose therefore showing upon the best authority we can find that everything we have alleged was in 1884 made the basis of Doctor Rowe's attack upon Mr. Buckell and other supporters of what Doctor Rowe characterised as a speculative breed. The late Doctor Rowe was for many years editor of the *American Field*, and his name still stands on its title page as its founder, which is not quite correct, as he took over a struggling paper some two or three years old and after a few years changed its name to *American Field*. To-day it is the staunchest supporter of the Llewellyn cult, and in the stud book which it publishes annually there is a section entitled Llewellyn Setters as distinguished from English Setters.

To paraphrase a well-known proverb, when fanciers fall out we are apt to hear some honest truths. At the close of the year 1883 Doctor Rowe announced that he would send some setter puppies he had bred on theoretical lines to compete at the English field trials. The result was quite a wordy warfare with some gentlemen he had been very friendly with in the matter of supporting the field trials strain. Mr. Buckell said he was not telling the truth and the Doctor claimed "he was rude and personal."

. . . "A contributor to *Land and Water* declared we had been guilty of an unsportsmanlike act in trying to appropriate the puppies as American-bred dogs; another declared we knew more about Kentucky widows than of breeding setters, and another pronounced us to be a feather-bed sportsman; our theories of breeding were declared vaporous effusions; the *Turf*,

Field and Farm assailed us and now Mr. L. H. Smith declares we are "a bottle of soda water," whereupon the Doctor uncorked himself and told more real truths about the Llewellyn business than has appeared in that paper since then. It is impossible to quote him in the entirety as what he had to say on the subject filled a score of pages from first to last, but the following extracts are pertinent:

"When a breeder by any peculiar plan shall change a breed of animals, and that change is uniform and can be intelligently defined, the group admits of a new classification. But Mr. Buckell (Mr. Llewellyn's right-hand man) ignores these facts when he writes about the Llewellyn setter as a breed. Neither he nor Mr. Llewellyn can show a title to the name, nor has any attempt been made to show what right Mr. Llewellyn has to monopolise the breeding of the dogs he calls Llewellyns. He bought Dan and Dick and Dora from their breeder Mr. Statter; then he purchased the Laverack setters Prince, Countess, Nellie, Lill II., and others. Dan, Dick and Dora he called Llewellyn setters. Dora's puppies by a Laverack dog he called Llewellyn setters. He might as well have called the Laverack setters Llewellyns. If he had a right to call Dan a Llewellyn setter, simply because he owned him, any man has the right to class any dog he may purchase as of a special new breed.

"But Mr. Llewellyn did not stop with so much monopoly as we have mentioned. He proclaimed, or Mr. Buckell did for him, that every dog in the land which was bred like Dan or Dick or Dora, or their progeny, out of Laverack setters were Llewellyn setters, and it mattered not where they were owned or who bred them. He went still further, and claimed as his breed all dogs out of Rhoebe (a bitch he did not breed or own) by a Laverack dog. Dogs by Duke (a dog he neither bred nor owned) out of a Laverack setter bitch were his breed; dogs by Duke out of Rhœbe were his breed; the progeny of Duke-Rhœbe on the Laveracks were his breed. These bred back again to the Laveracks or to the other side were his breed. It does not make any difference how much Laverack blood there might be in a dog if the remotest part of the pedigree shows Duke or Rhœbe, or Dan or Dora, or any of the many Duke-Rhœbe-Laverack combinations, they are his breed if no other blood is shown. On the other hand, it matters not how much Duke or Rhœbe blood, or both, is present, a drop of Laverack makes it Llewellyn.

"Thus Rob Roy, a noted field trial dog which Mr. Llewellyn never owned, a dog he did not breed, a dog whose ancestors he never owned nor bred, was according to Messrs. Buckell and Llewellyn, a Llewellyn setter, Rock, a field trial winner in England, bred by Mr. Garth, out of Daisy by Field's Bruce, was also a Llewellyn setter, according to Mr. Llewelyln's classification. Belton, the sire of Mr. Sanborn's crack field trial winner Nellie, was monopolised as a Llewellyn, yet he was bred by Mr. Thomas Statter, out of Daisy (not Llewellyn's), by Sykes's Dash, a Laverack setter. Mr. Brewis's celebrated Dash II., by Mr. Laverack's Blue Prince out of Mr. John Armstrong's Old Kate, is by Mr. Llewellyn claimed as his breed. His excellent brother Dash III. is also, according to Messrs. Buckell and Llewellyn, a Llewellyn setter; and we might go on at great length and show a long list of dogs, bred by others, from dogs not bred or owned by Mr. Llewellyn, which that gentleman claims as his breed, without a particle of reason.

"Had Mr. Llewellyn originated the Duke-Rhœbe-Laverack cross he might have some claim on the whole strain, but the cross was made, and its excellence proven before he owned any of them. Nor is Mr. Llewellyn entitled to any special recognition for having continued to breed these dogs exclusively, for they have been bred in England and in this country by others, during the whole time he has been breeding them.

"Has Mr. Llewellyn done all that it is claimed he has, and are all these dogs, whose performances go to swell the 'Llewellyn record' his dogs? Most assuredly not. He has no more right to their record than we have. What Mr. Laverack, Mr. Statter, Mr. Garth, Mr. Armstrong and others have done in England with their dogs, they, and not Mr. Llewellyn, are entitled to credit for. And what Mr. Smith, the Messrs. Bryson, Mr. Adams, Mr. Sanborn, Mr. Bergundthal, Mr. Higgins, Mr. Dew and many others have done in this country, they, and not Mr. Llewellyn, are entitled to credit for."—*American Field*, January 19, 1884.

Replying to a Canadian correspondent in the *American Field* of February 9, 1884, Doctor Rowe writes: "Dominion's assumptions, when brought face to face with facts, furnish striking evidence of the length and breadth of the claims of Mr. Llewellyn and his followers. Every dog that is of any consequence as a field trials performer gets to be a Llewellyn setter. A little investigation through the great mass of 'Llewellyn setter' assumption brings us to a very few commonplace facts."

When Mr. L. H. Smith, in the columns of the *Turf, Field and Farm,*

MR. E. H. BARRY'S ENGLISH SETTER CHAMPION QUEENS PRIDE

Winner of many prizes

160

took Doctor Rowe to task he was treated to a three-column reply, from which we take the following: "We have asked how it is that Dan is a Llewellyn setter when he is a Duke-Rhœbe and nothing else; how it is that dogs which are not Duke-Rhœbe can be Llewellyns; and how if Duke-Rhœbe-Laverack equals a Llewellyn, Duke-Laverack, or Rhœbe-Laverack can equal the same thing. The question was asked in all seriousness, and the reply is: 'Your statements are vaporous effusions'—'You know more about Kentucky widows than about breeding setters'—'You are a feather-bed sportsman' —'You are one of those talkative, effervescing little fellows'—'You are a bottle of soda water.'

"We now have another question to ask, and if Messrs. Buckell and Llewellyn cannot answer it, perhaps Mr. Smith can. Admitting that Mr. Llewellyn has a right to the title he claims, that all combinations of Duke-Rhœbe-Laverack are Llewellyns, how can he claim the progeny of Dash II. to be Llewellyns when they have other blood than that to which the so-called Llewellyn breed was limited by the definition? We can ask a great many other questions as difficult for Messrs. Buckell, Llewellyn and Smith to answer satisfactorily, but we have asked sufficient for the present; when Mr. Smith and his friends answer those which have been asked it will be time to ask the others."—*American Field*, May 10, 1884.

.   .   .   .

"We repeat Mr. Llewellyn has not any right to the title which he has claimed, and the idea that the term 'Llewellyn setter' has served as the exponent of a principle is absurd. In the first place, as we have said before, Mr. Llewellin was not the originator of the plan of breeding the setters he claims as his own; he borrowed it; Messrs. Statter and Field had bred in the manner Mr. Llewellyn began to breed before Mr. Llewellyn owned any one of the dogs which he afterward bred from.

"When we published the letters proposing that the title should be conferred on Mr. Llewellyn, we were asked to endorse the claim, which we positively refused to do and did not do for the reason that we did not consider Mr. Llewellyn entitled to it, and regarded it as cheap veneer, an imitation of Mr. Laverack." . . . "That we admitted the title to the dogs and styled them by it in our columns is not any more evidence that we endorsed it than that we endorsed it when we published the letters conferring the title. We received several private letters at the time asking if we approved of it, to which we replied we decidedly did not." . . . "The dogs were not then popular (1878), excepting among a few who owned them, consequently there were not those who, although they ridiculed the idea, yet took sufficient interest in the matter to oppose it quickly. The title therefor came into use, and we used it and admitted it into our columns the same as we did and do many other vulgarisms, as for instance the term prairie chicken for pinnated grouse."—*American Field*, April 26, 1884.

In the article last quoted from, Doctor Rowe said that Messrs. Buckell and Llewellyn were speculative breeders, by which he meant that they had no staple method, but brought in various outside blood. A correspondent replied to this and said that when he visited Mr. Llewellyn's kennels, in 1875, the dogs were a mixed lot. To his eyes, there were too many extremes in size and quality to show what was being bred for. In 1882 he again visited the kennels and found that there was a vast improvement. The dogs were larger and more of one definite type. Doctor Rowe twisted his correspondent's statements to suit what he had previously written and finishes his editorial foot-note to the letter with this sentence: "We know Mr. Llewellyn wrote Mr. A. H. Moore that he sent only his culls to America; that doubtless accounts for the evenness of the dogs described and the unevenness of those we have seen."

These were the pertinent and never answered statements of the editor of the most aggressive kennel journal in the country at that time, and they were penned when all the facts regarding the introduction and pedigrees as well as the giving the name were thoroughly well known to readers of kennel and sportsmen's papers. Now, at this late date, when so many of the actors in the events of that period are no more, and others are on the non-combatant list, searchers after truth are misled on every hand and seemingly have no option but to believe what was twenty years pilloried as erroneous and without foundation in fact. Even the *American Field* itself, regardless of the dictum of its old editor, has switched as the following from its issue of January 7, 1905, clearly shows: "It will be remembered that a protest was made against awarding the special prize of twenty-five dollars, offered by Mr. J. A. Graham for the best straightbred [this is incorrect, there was nothing as to straightbred in the conditions announced regarding the special, simply best Llewellyn setter dog] at the World's Fair to Bracken O'Leck. The matter was referred to the *American Field*, and it decided that Bracken O'Leck is not a Llewellyn setter, for the very reason that he

162

MR. RIPLINGER'S ENGLISH SETTER BITCH PERA

Photo by Schreiber

A prominent Eastern winner before being sent to Mr. Riplinger's Seattle kennels

MR. RIPLINGER'S ENGLISH SETTER ELLOREE

Photo by Schreiber

Also a leading winner at Eastern dog shows, now at Seattle, Wash.

has blood in his veins other than the Duke-Rhœbe-Kate-Laverack." Of course, not being confined to those lines, he could not be a "Llewellyn." That is true enough, but if his breeding had been within those lines the decision would have been the other way; a way that Doctor Rowe would not have decided it in 1884, when he said Mr. Llewellyn had not a particle of reason to claim the Kate line, even admitting the Duke-Rhœbe-Laverack, which was merely a borrowed idea from older breeders.

There is a virtue in choosing your own referee as was done in this case, and that reminds us of a still more sudden reversal of opinions. About 1874 C. J. Foster was supplanted as editor of the *Spirit of the Times* by Mr. J. H. Saunders, who had had little experience in the then important duty on sporting papers of deciding wagers. The result was that he reversed certain rulings which had for years been taken advantage of by clever betters, who knew that the *Spirit* decided one way and the *Clipper* the reverse. One was the value of a certain throw with dice, and this Mr. Saunders changed to the *Clipper* decision, and the loser came to us about it, as we were then on the paper. Our advice was to follow the ruling of the new editor and have another question referred to the *Spirit*. And this he did, but in the meanwhile Mr. Saunders had received so many letters calling his attention to the "error" that when the question cropped up next week he went back to the old decision, and the twice loser came in hot haste with the paper containing it. The advice this time was to mark both papers and send them with a note to Mr. George Wilkes, the proprietor, with a statement of the facts. This he did, and Wilkes, knowing the importance of this department of the paper, at once sent his check for the hundred dollars, with a strong expression of regret; then he had a talk with Mr. Saunders, and the department was turned over to us to run on the familiar lines on all questions, except to formally state that the decision regarding the man and the squirrel in the tree was to be changed, and after that the man never walked around the squirrel, dodging on the opposite side, at least in the *Spirit's* columns.

Had Doctor Rowe been as firm a man as George Wilkes he would have got rid of the term Llewellyn, just as George Wilkes stamped out timing fractions in trotting records. These would be reported in fifths and other fractions, but the office rule was that quarters could alone be used, and every report was changed to conform therewith. Other papers copied the *Spirit*, and sportsmen after that would buy only quarter-second timing watches. To be consistent, Doctor Rowe should have copied Stonehenge and called these setters Dan-Laveracks and altered the term Llewellyn in every published communication, but unfortunately he did not.

Points of a Good Setter

The many excellent illustrations we give of dogs known for their good points is a far better education than any supposed-to-be typical drawing. In all dogs there are possibilities of improvement, and in some of our illustrations of even the best dogs the reader, if he possesses the eye for symmetry and proportion, will be able to detect faults in conformation. They are also vastly superior to attempting to educate by the "standard" alone, however clear the description of what is desirable may be. By taking the standard and looking carefully at the illustrations, point by point, the seeker for light will surely reach the desired end. There have been several standards, more than one having been made to fit certain dogs and foist a totally wrong type of setter upon breeders. Very fortunately, these never met with support, each in turn being dropped, and the one which was lately adopted by breeders and exhibitors of the correct type, is short, concise and readily understood. It is that adopted by the English Setter Club of America:

"*Head.*—Should be long and lean, with a well-defined stop. The skull oval from ear to ear, showing plenty of brain room, and with a well-defined occipital protuberance. The muzzle moderately deep and fairly square; from the stop to the point of the nose should be long, the nostrils wide, and the jaws of equal length; flews not to be pendulous, but of sufficient depth to give a squareness to the muzzle; the colour of the nose should be black, or dark, or light liver, according to the colour of the coat. The eyes should be bright, mild, and intelligent, and of a dark hazel colour—the darker the better. The ears of moderate length, set on low and hanging in neat folds close to the cheek; the tip should be velvety, the upper part clothed with fine silky hair.

"*Neck.*—Should be rather long, muscular and lean, slightly arched at the crest, and clean cut where it joins the head; toward the shoulder it should be larger and very muscular, not throaty, though the skin is loose below the throat, elegant and blood-like in appearance.

"*Body.*—Should be of moderate length, with shoulders well set back,

JUDGING A VARIETY CLASS AT THE LADIES' KENNEL ASSOCIATION SHOW AT MINEOLA, L. I., 1904

166

or oblique; back short and level; loins wide, slightly arched, strong and muscular. Chest deep in the brisket, with ribs well sprung back of elbows with good depth of back ribs.

"*Legs and Feet.*—Stifles well bent and strong, thighs long from hip to hock. The forearm big and very muscular, the elbow well let down. Pastern short, muscular and straight. The feet very close and compact, and well protected by hair between the toes.

"*Tail.*—The tail should be set on slightly below the line of the back, almost in a line with the back, to be carried straight from the body, a curve in any direction objectionable; should not extend below the hocks when brought down, shorter more desirable, not curly or ropy; the flag or feather hanging in long pendant flakes. The feather should not commence at root, but slightly below, and increase in length to the middle, then gradually taper off toward the end; and the hair long, bright, soft and silky, wavy but not curly.

"*Symmetry, Coat and Feathering.*—The coat should be straight, long and silky (a slight wave admissible), which should be the case with the breeches and forelegs, which, nearly down to the feet, should be well feathered.

"*Colour and Markings.*—The colour may be either white and black, white and orange, white and lemon, white and liver, or tri-colour, that is, white, black and tan; those without heavy patches of colour on the body, but flecked all over, preferred."

Scale of Points

Head	20	Tail	5
Neck	5	Symmetry, coat and	
Body	25	feathering	20
Legs and feet	20	Colour and Markings	5
Total			100

167

SETTERS, ENGLISH (Canis Index).

THE exact period of the introduction to this country of "The Setter" (in early times called the Spaniel or Setting dog) is uncertain. That the "Setter" and "Spaniel" were originally identical few will dispute.

THE ENGLISH SETTER (showing Keepers drawing the net).
Engraved from an original picture in the possession of Mr. Bradford,
1782, the engraving in the possession of the General Editor.

It is recorded that so early as 1555 Robert Dudley, Duke of Northumberland, trained a Setter to the net; thus, in these early times the breed was in existence and most probably a considerable time previously.

The work of the Setter in those days was to point the birds (Partridges and Quails) and to "Sit" or "Crouch," and thus remain, allowing the net to be drawn up to him and the birds taken in it. We also read of the Setter or Spaniel trained to flush the game at which the hunter flew his hawks. This latter work seems to correspond with that of "The Spaniel" as we know him to-day, and the former to the work of our present-day Setters and Pointers, the gun, of course, taking the place of the net and hawks.

Gervase Markham, writing in 1655 ("The Art of Fowling") says:—" To speake then in a word touching the best choice of this "Setting-dogge let him be as neere as you can the best bredde land-"spaniell that you can procure: and though some have been curious "in observing of their colours, as giving preheminence to the Motley, "the lieur-hude or the white and blacke spotted."

Much earlier reference has been made to the "Spaniel or Setting dogge" than those above mentioned, but, for the purposes of so short an article as this, it does not appear necessary to go further into this ancient history.

Coming to later times—In the year 1814 a book, "Kunopædia," was published, written by William Dobson, Esq., of Eden Hall, Cumberland, being instructions for breaking Setters and Pointers. As the title of this work shows that in 1814 the Setter was known by the name of Spaniel, I give here a copy of it, which is also interesting as showing that the art of "Shooting Flying" was beginning to be practised, or, at any rate, a not very well known achievement. The title of the book is

" 'KUNOPÆDIA,'

" A practical essay on breaking or training the *English Spaniel or* "*Pointer*, with instructions for attaining the art of shooting flying, in "in which the latter is reduced to rule and the former inculcated on "principle."

170

The instructions given for breaking or training in this work are those to teach the dog to point, and generally to range and hunt as our modern Pointers and Setters do ; and not as the name "English Spaniel" would suggest to hunt, as our Spaniels do to-day.

It is a fact that even at the present time the older generation of keepers and others refer to the Setter as the "Spanell" or "Spanell Dog" in Cumberland and other parts of the North of England.

Colonel Hawker, in his excellent work on all that relates to shooting, and especially to wild-fowl shooting ("Instructions to Young Sportsmen") gives a very limited space to the consideration of dogs employed in Field Sports.

Setters as a class are divided into three distinct breeds, viz. :—

1. *The Black and Tan, or Gordon.*
2. *The English.*
3. *The Irish.*

THE ENGLISH SETTER.

This division of the "Setter" is again sub-divided into many different strains, known in some instances by the name of their owner, or of the locality in which they have been bred, but as in the space of this short history of the breed there is not room to enumerate all of them, and, as in fact, they all come under the common family name, "The English Setter," it will suffice to mention a few only of the more important strains which are known to us to-day.

To Mr. Edward Laverack, who was born at Keswick, Cumberland, in 1800, and who died at Ash, near Whitchurch, Shropshire, in 1877, the present-day English Setter owes much. The writer cannot do better than quote the late Mr. Rawdon B. Lee's opinion upon this point.

In his very interesting book, "Modern Dogs," referring to Mr. Laverack, Mr. Lee says :—

"Without doubt to the late Mr. Edward Laverack, who died in "April, 1877, the present generation is indebted for the excellence of "the Setter, both in form and work, as he is found to-day, and with "few exceptions the very best dogs are actual descendants of the "Laverack strain."

This breed of Setter is often known by the name of "The Laverack Setter"; it is in reality a pure bred English Setter, bearing the name of Mr. Laverack, who kept and bred it as a particular strain for very many years. There is no doubt that Setters of this Laverack blood, both for excellence in the field, endurance, and good looks, are very hard to beat.

Mr. Laverack kept and used his dogs for work; he rented extensive moors in Scotland and the North of England. Also on the introduction of Dog Shows he exhibited his Setters with great success, as can be seen by reference to the Kennel Club. Stud books of that period.

He was a firm believer in pedigree and keeping the blood pure, and breeding for those necessary qualifications for work in the field— endurance and nose.

This breed of Setters (so the owner tells us) was started in the year 1825, on his purchasing from the Rev. A. Harrison, near Carlisle, who bred them, "Old Moll" and "Ponto"; and from these two he bred his famous strain.

When Mr. Laverack obtained these two dogs in 1825 they were then of the pure strain for 35 years, which takes us back to the year 1790, and as Mr. Laverack kept up a pure strain from these for over 44 years it makes a continuous blood for 80 years.

In 1872 Mr. Laverack, when he was over 73 years of age, wrote a book, "The Setter," a work which was long ago out of print, and at the present time difficult to obtain. In it he thus describes the Setter:

"Of all sporting dogs, perhaps, there are none more generally "useful, beautiful and sagacious than the Setter.

"That the Setter is the most generally useful of shooting dogs I "fancy few will deny, being possessed of more lasting powers of "endurance, therefore, better adapted for all localities and weathers. "The Setter can stand cold or heat alike; the hair on his feet and "between his toes allows him to hunt rough cover as well as the "Spaniel—in fact, the Setter is but an improved Spaniel."

Again he says, speaking of his own dogs, "It is a fact that I have "run dogs of this breed for three weeks daily from 9 a.m. to 7 p.m., "and others possessing the same blood have done the same."

172

Mr. Laverack bred and kept a considerable number of Setters, and appears, also, to have sold many, both in England and Scotland.

Some of his best known dogs were Dash, Blue Prince, Blue Dash, Cora, Fred IV., Sting, and numerous others. In his book Mr. Laverack gives us an illustration of the Setter " Dash " at the age of 10 years ; a somewhat heavy looking, blue-ticked dog, showing a great amount of throatiness ; of course, this may be accounted for by his age.

Below is the pedigree of this dog, " Dash," going back to the original " Ponto " and " Old Moll."

All the above-mentioned dogs, except "Old Moll" and " Ponto," were bred by Mr. Laverack.

Speaking of the colour of this Laverack strain of Setter, the owner mentions "Black Greys " or " Flints," " Blue Beltons " or " Lemon and White Beltons," being the same colours we have in the present day patterns.

The Black Greys or Flints are what we would call a blue roan now, a very taking colour when the whole body and head are the same colour and no patches.

- **Dash 2nd**
  - Sting
    - Rock 2nd
      - Regent
        - Pilot — Dash 1st / Belle 1st
        - Moll 2nd — Dash 1st / Belle 1st
      - Jet 1st
        - Pilot — Dash 1st / Belle 1st
        - Moll 2nd — Dash 1st / Belle 1st
    - Cora (Blairs)
      - Regent
        - Pilot — Dash 1st / Belle 1st
        - Moll 2nd — Dash 1st / Belle 1st
      - Jet 1st
        - Pilot — Dash 1st / Belle 1st
        - Moll 2nd — Dash 1st / Belle 1st
  - Cora
    - Fred 1st
      - Rock
        - Rock — Pilot / Moll 2nd
        - Peg — Dash 1st / Moll 2nd
      - Moll 2nd
        - Dash 1st — Ponto / Old Moll
        - Belle 1st — Ponto / Old Moll
    - Cora 1st
      - Dash 1st — Ponto / Old Moll
      - Belle 1st — Ponto / Old Moll

- **Moll 3rd**
  - Fred 1st
    - Rock 1st
      - Rock
        - Pilot — Dash 1st / Belle 1st
        - Moll 2nd — Dash 1st / Belle 1st
      - Peg
        - Dash 1st — Ponto / Old Moll
        - Moll 2nd — Dash 1st / Belle 1st
    - Moll 2nd
      - Dash 1st — Ponto / Old Moll
      - Belle 1st — Ponto / Old Moll
  - Belle 2nd
    - Rock 2nd
      - Regent
        - Pilot — Dash 1st / Belle 1st
        - Moll 2nd — Dash 1st / Belle 1st
      - Jet 1st
        - Pilot — Dash 1st / Belle 1st
        - Moll 2nd — Dash 1st / Belle 1st
    - Cora (Blairs)
      - Regent
        - Pilot — Dash 1st / Belle 1st
        - Moll 2nd — Dash 1st / Belle 1st
      - Jet 1st
        - Pilot — Dash 1st / Belle 1st
        - Moll 2nd — Dash 1st / Belle 1st

" *Field*."   *30th June, 1906.*

EDWARD LAVERACK.

On the right hand side of the road as you are going from Whitchurch to the village of Ash, in Shropshire, there is a small red brick house with stabling and outbuildings. I have passed Broughall Cottage many times, and knew it as a hunting box owned by a follower of Sir Watkin Wynn's hounds and neighbouring packs. Not until recently was I aware it was the place where Edward Laverack lived and bred his setters. Within a stone's throw of where I am writing is Ash Church, and a frequent walk is to go over the stile, round the churchyard, and through the fields to Ash Parva. It is impossible to pass this little churchyard without noting a tall tombstone. The other day I stopped to read what was on this stone, and found the following:

To the memory of Edward Laverack; born Keswick, 1800; died at Broughall Cottage, 1877. This monument is erected by admirers in England and America.

This is the only monument to my knowledge ever erected by the friends of a breeder of sporting dogs by reason of his fame in two great countries. Maybe others have been equally ignorant of the memento paid to Laverack, but that I should have scores and scores of times almost walked over his grave without knowing it is much against me.

On the other side of the stone is written:

His great love for the lower animals made him many friends. He was especially fond of dogs, and by careful selection remodelled the English setter, the best of which are known by his name.

" He prayeth well who loveth well, both man, and bird, and beast."

Whilst I was copying the above words there came across the fields the sound of canine voices, and in the still of the evening a full chorus floated over the churchyard. Could Laverack have heard he would have known that sound. It was from the gun dogs at Ightfield— Major Heywood-Lonsdale's. But those palatial kennels at Ightfield were not erected until some years after Laverack had died. They were built about the time Brailsford—a name familiar to readers of the *Field*— took over the management of the late Mr. Heywood-Lonsdale's dogs, an uncle to the present owner. What would Laverack have thought of such kennels? Erected at a cost of £2,000, they are indeed palatial, compared to those existing at Broughall Cottage over half a century ago. What was done at that time for the English setter is well known, but some interesting facts are yet to be got from one or two of the old villagers at Ash. Old Dan Cliff, for instance, whose smithy stands by the school, knew Laverack well; but his anvil does not clang as often as it once did. Providence seems to have been hard on Dan.

J. A. TATHAM.

Our English Setter Club, which was established in 1890, issues a description of the points of this breed, and, as it is almost the same as that given by Mr. Laverack, the Setter Club's description is given here :—

DESCRIPTION OF THE ENGLISH SETTER.

Head—Should be long and lean, with a well-defined stop. The skull oval from ear to ear, showing plenty of brain room, and with a well-defined occipital protuberance. The muzzle moderately deep and fairly square ; from the stop to the point of the nose should be long, the nostrils wide and the jaws of nearly equal length, flews not to be pendulous ; the colour of the nose should be black or dark, or light liver, according to the colour of the coat. The eyes should be bright, mild and intelligent, and of a dark hazel colour, the darker the better. The ears of moderate length, set on low and hanging in neat folds close to the cheek ; the tip should be velvety, the upper part clothed with fine silky hair. *Neck*—Should be rather long, muscular and lean, slightly arched at the crest and clean cut where it joins the head ; towards the shoulder it should be larger and very muscular, not throaty or any pendulosity below the throat, but elegant and blood-like in appearance. *Body*—Should be of moderate length, with shoulders well set back, or oblique ; back short and level, loins wide, slightly arched, strong and muscular. Chest deep in the brisket, with good, round, widely sprung ribs, deep in the back ribs ; that is, well ribbed up. *Legs and Feet.*—Stifles well bent and ragged, thighs long from hip to hock. The forearm big and very muscular, the elbow well let down. Pasterns short, muscular and straight. The feet very close and compact, and well protected by hair between the toes. *Tail*—The tail should be set on almost in a line with the back ; medium length, not curly or ropy, to be slightly curved or scimitar-shaped, but with no tendency to turn upwards, the flag or feather hanging in long pendant flakes. The feather should not commence at the root, but slightly below, and increase in length to the middle, then gradually taper off towards the end ; and the hair long, bright, soft and silky, wavy, but not curly. *Coat and Feathering*—The Coat, from the back of the head in a line with the ears, ought to be slightly

176

wavy, long and silky, which should be the case with the coat generally; the breeches and forelegs nearly down to the feet should be well feathered. *Colour and Markings*—The colour may be either Black and White, Lemon and White, Liver and White, or Tricolour, that is, Black, White and Tan; those without heavy patches of colour on the body, but flecked all over, preferred.

This standard, as previously mentioned, is practically identical with Mr. Laverack's description. Possibly, about the time of Laverack's "Dash" (in the late sixties and early seventies) the best dogs running at trials and exhibited at Shows were, to mention only a very few, Mr. Garth's "Q.C.," "Daisy," Mr. Purcell Llewellin's "Countess" and "Nellie," and Mr. Dickin's "Belle," and, no doubt, several other first-rate ones whose names do not occur to me now.

As "Dog Shows" and "Field Trials" were quite a new introduction towards the end of Mr. Laverack's time, it would not be out of place to give here a short extract from his opinion of each of these forms of public competition. With regard to Dog Shows he writes: —" I consider them a step in the right direction if honestly and honourably carried out without favouritism (which I think it is by the majority), and the judges competent," and later he says—" It is an undoubted fact that the major part of the sporting dogs exhibited have never been tested on game, but are merely specimens of external form." This is so at the present time, and in a still greater degree than when Laverack wrote. However, recently the Kennel Club have introduced a new rule, which does not allow a sporting dog (Pointer, Setter, Spaniel or Retriever) to become a full champion until it has passed some kind of a test to show that it is possessed of certain qualifications which will enable it to perform the work which is expected from it in the field. This is a step in the right direction, and will be welcomed by all who show dogs and who do not wish to see these beautiful breeds of sporting dogs degenerate into animals merely to look at on the benches of a Show; and, for the purposes of the work for which they have been used for centuries, become worthless. On the other hand, we must also look to the type and character of the breed, and keep up its good looks as well as its sporting instincts, and if the Field Trial dog of to-day, before he is allowed to become a full champion (as a Field Trial Winner) was compelled to pass some test as to looks and breed which would qualify him to enter a Show ring amongst good specimens of his own breed, it would be a further step in the right direction, and we then should see more good looking dogs at the Field Trials and more good workers on the Show Bench. With regard to Mr. Laverack's opinion of Field Trials, he agreed with them to a certain extent, but recommended Autumn Trials, so that game could be killed over the dogs, so that they could have longer trials of endurance and be tested on several kinds of game.

Another strain of English Setter was the "Naworth Castle Breed," an old strain in the possession of the Earls of Carlisle. This breed was easily distinguishable through having a slight "top knot" similar to that of the Irish Water Spaniel, but, of course, not so pronounced. A few specimens are seen at the present day, but they are rare. In colour they are liver and white, sometimes nearly pure white.

The next strain I shall refer to is that bred by Mr. R. L. Purcell Llewellin, and known by the name of "Llewellin Setters" in many places. This strain, which has been very carefully bred by Mr. Llewellin for a great number of years, has an excellent and almost unparalleled record both at Field Trials and on the Show Bench. From 1868 up to the present year, 1910 (when dogs from this kennel competed successfully in the Spring Trials) this strain has always held its own at both Shows and Trials. But in late years they have rarely been exhibited at Shows; a few years ago there were a very nice team of them shown at Shrewsbury, and they have often been seen at the Trials. It would take up too much room to go through the actual wins and performances of all the good animals that have come from this kennel, and as their records are chronicled in the Kennel Club Stud Books, mention only of a few of the best dogs will be made :—Dan, Quince, Countess Nellie, Ruby, Daisy, Countess Bear, Countess Moll, Count Wind'em, Rosa Wind'em, Floss Llewellin, Freda Llewellin, and Fairy Llewellin.

This strain of Setter is very highly thought of as a gun-dog, both in this country and America, and to the latter country a fair number of good specimens have gone.   Mr. Llewellin originally started with pure Laveracks, which he crossed with dogs from the kennels of Sir Vincent Corbet and Mr. T. Statter, of Manchester. Mr. Laverack dedicated his book, " The Setter," "to Mr. Llewellin, " who has endeavoured, and is still endeavouring, by sparing neither " expense nor trouble to bring to perfection the Setter." This breed must now have been in existence over forty years.

The next strain of Setter to be mentioned is that bred by the late Mr. James Birkett Cockerton, of Ravensbarrow Lodge, Grange-over-Sands, North Lancashire, between the years 1880-1900. This strain has played a very important part in the history of the Setter in recent years, and more especially in that of the Show Setter. These dogs were invariably good-looking, handsome, specimens of the breed, and, although not used for Field Trial work, were excellent in the field and regularly used for work by their owner.

With regard to their performances at Shows—although Mr. Cockerton was breeding Setters in the early seventies, he does not appear to have done much showing until about the year 1880 or 1881, but from that date up to nearly 1900 this kennel must have accounted for a great percentage of the prizes offered at shows. Most of our modern Setters have this strain in their pedigree.

Some of Mr. Cockerton's best dogs were : Monk of Furness (sold for a large price to Canada), Belle of Furness, Madam Rachel, Ellen Terry, Sir Simon, Cash in Hand, Buxom Maiden, Real Tory, Lord Bentinck, Lady Bentinck, Shylock, and Guy.   Mr. Laverack used to shoot in the neighbourhood of Grange, and Mr. Cockerton's dogs had a considerable amount of the Laverack Setter blood in them.

About this time there were many people about Kendal in Westmorland (not very far from Grange) breeding Setters of this same strain ; two, who were very successful, were the late Mr. G. Cartmell, of Eden Mount, Kendal, and the late Mr. W. Hartley, of New Road, Kendal.   Mr. Cartmell will be remembered as the owner of Royal Rock, Royal Sam, Sir Tatton, Carlton Frank and Carlton Madam, all well known on the Show Bench.   Mr. William Hartley bred some very good ones.   Amongst his best may be mentioned Lord Westmorland, Lady Westmorland, Richmond and Lord Romney (both

179

sold to the late Mr. R. B. Lee), Barton Tory, also sold to the same gentleman, who sold him to Sir H. F. De Trafford, and Monk O'Leck, which the writer bought from Mr. Hartley.

Mr. J. Shorthose was also the owner of some very nice Setters about 1880; he lived at Newcastle-upon-Tyne, and showed Novel (bred by Mr. Cockerton in 1877), Royal IV., Royalty, and Novelty.

That famous stud dog, "Sir Alister," owned by the late Mr. T. Cunnington, must be mentioned here; he was certainly one of the best sires of modern times. He was said to be rather a small dog and not a very handsome one, but his success at the stud cannot be disputed. Amongst those of which he was sire are Sir Simon, Count Howard, Sir Daniel, Monk of Furness, Queen Elsie, Lord Westmorland, and many other good ones.

"Sir Alister" was by Mr. G. Lowe's "Tam O'Shanter," *ex* Daisy.

Other well-known breeders of the English Setter were Messrs. Lort, Sir R. Garth, Q.C., Messrs. James and Elias Bishop, Barclay Field, A. P. Lonsdale, T. Pilkington (the owner of those well-known dogs "Lill" and "Dash"), Major Platt, Messrs. Armstrong (whose "Old Kate" is an ancestress of many of our best Setters), Lloyd Price, Bowers, Rev. J. C. Macdona (owner of the Lemon and White dog "Ranger"), Viscount Downe, the late Mr. George Lowe (who about 1877 owned that good dog, "Tam O'Shanter," by "Rock," *ex* "Rum"), Mr. F. C. Lowe (who has had many good Setters in his kennel, such as "Aldon Tam," "Grouse of Kippen," "Mabel of Kippen," "Cherry Picker," and others), Mr. J. Fletcher's "Rock" (4280), about the year 1877, was a noted dog, being particularly successful at stud; Mr. J. H. Salter, of Witham, Essex, has had some good Setters, and also Mr. T. Webber, of Falmouth.

We now come to a time when the Show Setter and the working animal are of two quite distinct types, and this difference in appearance is more marked each year, and, as has been before pointed out, it is quite unusual for an English Setter winning a Field Trial to be placed at all in the prize-list at a show, and *vice versâ*, for the prize-winner at the show to be placed at the trials. In fact, there are classes provided at the shows exclusively for

Setters having won some distinction at Field Trials, and until recently stakes were provided at the Trials, in which only prize-winners at a show could compete. This stake has, however, been abolished. Such a division should be quite unnecessary, for it ought to be quite possible to have a Setter possessing sufficient character and good looks to place it high up in the prize list at the show, and also the necessary working qualities to enable it to take a good position in the stake at the Trials. As before mentioned, this has been done by Mr. Purcell Llewellin's dogs some years ago, and doubtless by others also.

The kennel of English Setters of Mr. G. Potter, of Carlisle, is the next in order we come to, and some very handsome animals have been bred by him. Mr. Potter started breeding Setters in the early "eighties," and in the year 1884 he bred a very remarkable litter; they were by the late Mr. Cunnington's "Sir Alister" (before referred to) from Mr. Potter's "Mena." This litter consisted of "Count Howard," a champion and winner of many prizes both in England and America, he being sold to Mr. F. Windholz in the latter country. "Cora of Wetheral," another, was claimed by the same American gentleman on her first appearance at a show (Sheffield). She very soon became a champion on the other side. "Queen Elsie," another of the same litter, a champion and winner of many prizes both in this country and at Continental shows. She was claimed at Brussels Show, where, with her son, Champion "Geltsdale" and two others of the same family, she won the trophy for the best team of sporting dogs, the same team having won a similar honour at Roubaix the previous week. "Sir Gilbert," of the same litter, sold to France, where he won many prizes, eventually becoming a champion. "Carlisle," the last of this litter, was purchased by Mr. Elias Bishop, for whom he won many prizes—not a bad record for one family.

Amongst others that Mr. Potter has bred or owned were Champion "Geltsdale," born in 1887, and a constant winner from 1888 to 1891, "Wetheral Jet," and "Wetheral Gilbert"; he still keeps up this strain at the present time, his latest well-known dog, "Wetheral Pan," who, though still a puppy, has won four firsts at

Cruft's, two firsts and challenge at Manchester, and first at Ayr, 1910.

Mr. Potter is the Hon. Secretary of "the English Setter Club," which post he has held since the formation of the club in 1890; the objects of this club being to promote the breeding of pure English Setters; to define and publish a description of the true type; to urge the adoption of such type on breeders, judges, etc., as the standard of excellence by which the English Setter should be judged; to promote Field Trials; to offer prizes for competition at Dog Shows and Field Trials to members of the Club and to adopt such other means as may be deemed advisable for the encouragement of the breed. The club also holds a two-days Field Trial Meeting (open in some stakes to Setters of all breeds and to Pointers) in the spring of each year, and offers prizes at both Shows and Trials to its members.

A club on these lines has lately been formed in New Zealand for the encouragement of the breeding of Pointers and Setters, to which all English fanciers will wish success.

Undoubtedly one of the best kennels of English Setters existing to-day is that of Mr. T. Steadman, of Mallwyd, Dinas Mawddwy, Merionethshire. Mr. Steadman first started this kennel at Appleby in Westmorland, where he lived previously to moving to Wales. He has been breeding Setters since 1870, but did not begin to show them until some time in the "eighties." The first litter Mr. Steadman bred were from a bitch of a strain that had been owned by his family for very many years, long before Dog Shows were known, all of this strain being kept entirely for work. This bitch he mated to Champion "Royal Rock," belonging to the late Mr. L. Hartley, of Kendal. This was the start of the kennel, the success of which on the Show Bench for a great number of years is so well known; and the writer believes, with very few (if any) exceptions, the inmates of this kennel are all trained to work. He has himself seen a number of them on game, and a more successful team of good looking Setters to shoot over would be difficult to find.

Amongst some of the best bred at Mallwyd (and previously at Appleby) are "Countess of Appleby," "Olinda," "Pansy Blossom,"

"Simonian," "Mallwyd Beatrice," "Mallwyd Flo" (sold to Sir H. F. De Trafford), Champion "Mallwyd Bess" (also sold to the Barton Kennels for 200 guineas); this bitch later came into the writer's possession and remained with him until her death, and was probably the best Setter seen in the last 20 years. "Mallwyd Prince," "Mallwyd Ben," Champion "Mallwyd Don," Champion

" MEG O'LECK."
Now in America.

"Mallwyd Belle," Champion "Mallwyd Sirdar" (claimed at Birmingham Show by Mr. P. Heaton, for £100, who afterwards sent him to America, where he has quite recently died), Champion "Mallwyd Sarah" (winner of many prizes, and sent to America), "Mallwyd Rebecca," Champion "Mallwyd Mumm," Champion "Mallwyd

Rock," Champion " Mallwyd Ned" (three litter brothers), " Mallwyd Nell," " Mallwyd Diamond " (a champion), " Mallwyd Catherine," and " Mallwyd Violet." This latter, " Mallwyd Violet," Mr. Steadman considers the best Setter he has bred during the many years he has kept them. Mr. Steadman also keeps a considerable number of Pointers, and occasionally runs both these and his Setters at the Trials.

The writer may here mention a few of the best Setters he has owned or bred during the last twenty years. They are " Sir Reuben" (a liver and white dog, who won many prizes from

CH. " MALLWYD SARAH."

1890-93), " Mallwyd Flo," " Heather John " (a very good stud dog), Champion " Mallwyd Bess," " Barton Maud," " Rhoda O'Leck," " Flash O'Leck " (sent to Kimberley, South Africa, in 1900), " Fan O'Leck," " Flirt O'Leck " (two lemon and white sisters, both in America), " Rose O'Leck," " Princess Evelyn " (the dam of Champion " Mallwyd Sailor" and Champion " Mallwyd Sarah"), " Moll O'Leck," " Meg O'Leck," and " Fly O'Leck " (these three bitches were sold to Mr. B. Lewis, Philadelphia, U.S.A., where they are now all Champions), Champion " Monk O'Leck," Champion " Fur

O'Leck," and "Feather O'Leck" (now in the possession of Sir Archibald Campbell, Inverarary). The above Setters were all prize-winners at the best shows and many of them very useful in the field.

Sir H. F. De Trafford had a very good lot of English Setters (along with the many other breeds he kept) both Show dogs and Field Trial winners. The best of his Show Setters were Champion "Barton Tory," Champion "Mallwyd Bess," "Mallwyd Flo," "Barton Maud," his best Field Trial dogs in English Setters being

CH. " MONK O'LECK."

" Barton Charmer " and " Grouse of Kippen." The whole of this kennel (including Pointers, English and Irish Setters, etc.), was sold by auction at Aldridge's in 1898.

The Messrs. Bottomley, of Bradford, also about this time exhibited many good English Setters, as did Mr. G. Pridmore, of Coleshill, Warwickshire. Mr. J. Poole, of Ulverston, showed those two good blue-ticked dogs, " Ulverston Rock " and " Ulverston Ranger."

185

Mr. H. E. Gray, of Brecon, has turned out many good animals his "Vanguard," "Electra," "Brettina," and "Destiny" being the best known.

Mr. E. Cockill, of Gomersal, has been a regular exhibitor and breeder of English Setters for a considerable number of years, and has been very successful. His best known ones are "Idris," "Mallwyd Bob," Champion "Mallwyd Sailor" and Champion "Broomhill Betsy," a bitch who has had a most successful career, and is now only in her prime, and is a very handsome Setter.

CH. "FUR O'LECK."

Mr. George Raper, of Gomersal, has almost always found room in his great variety team of dogs for a good English Setter, owning, amongst others, those good dogs, Champion "Barton Tory," Champion "Mallwyd Bess," "Rockaway," and "Mallwyd Rock."

Mr. J. J. Holgate's lemon and white, Champion "Mallwyd Ned," has won a great number of prizes, and is a very typical Setter.

Mr. H. Gunn, of Cardiff, who will be chiefly remembered as the breeder of Champion "Rumney Rock," "Rumney Racket," and later of that nice bitch, Champion "Rumney Radiance," has a select

186

kennel of Setters. "Radiance" has followed many of our best Setters to America, where she is still winning prizes. There are, no doubt, many good Setters which could have been added to this list had space allowed.

We must now leave the Show Setters and turn to some of the best of those who have distinguished themselves in the field.

Field Trials have always been very popular, but at no time more so than they are to-day, and each year more owners are having their best Setters trained for these meetings, of which there are no

CH. "BROOMHILL BETSY."

less than eight separate ones for Pointers and Setters, besides numerous others for Retrievers and Spaniels.

The Trials for Pointers and Setters are:—The International Gun Dog League (Brace Stakes), and the Kennel Club Meeting (both for many years held near Ipswich); the English Setter Club Trials (run for the last two years at Oundle, in Northamptonshire, by the kind permission of Lord Lilford); the National Trials at Shrewsbury; the Pembrokeshire Club Meeting; The International Gun Dog League (on grouse in August), near Lanark, N.B. The Pointer Club (also on grouse) at Shap, Westmorland, in July, 1909

187

(no meeting in 1910); the Irish Red Setter Club Trials (on grouse), held in 1909 in Co. Wicklow, and in 1910 in Co. Donegal. There is generally a very good entry at all these meetings, the prizes offered being very substantial, besides the additional value placed on the dogs winning prizes in any of the stakes.

Dealing with the Field Trial dogs as a class, although equally good in their work as formerly, they cannot be said to have retained their good looks and Setter character. There does not appear to be

"LINGFIELD NELL."

any definite standard or type, and any dog that shows he can work runs whatever his looks may happen to be. This remark is only intended to apply to these working Setters as a class, for, of course, there are many exceptions. With regard to the working of these dogs, there seems to be better and more careful work done at the Trials now than even a few years ago; one very rarely sees a bad dog in the whole of the entries, and nothing is more interesting than to see the great amount of intelligence shown by these dogs when at work. It would be quite impossible to refer to each of these trials and the Setters individually that have run well in them, so only some of the chief kennels that have generally been to the front can be here noticed.

The names of James and Elias Bishop have been known for a very long time in connection with Field Trials, both of them having had a good share of success with the Pointers and Setters they have run; Mr. R. Ll. P. Llewellin has been previously referred to; Captain Heywood Lonsdale, the owner of the famous Ightfield

"LINGFIELD BERYL."

kennel of English Setters in Shropshire (the kennel which was formerly in charge of that well-known breaker, Brailsford, now of Cameron), is generally represented at the chief meetings successfully; so also is Colonel C. J. Cotes, of Pitchford, near Shrewsbury, whose dogs, both Pointers, Setters and Retrievers, have done such good work for many years, the owner nearly always being present at each meeting; these dogs are handled by Tirrell. Mr. B. J. Warwick has always sent some of the best working Setters to these Trials, some of the best known being " Compton Sam," " Compton Bounce," " Compton Sandy," " Compton Minnie," and the blue-ticked and tan bitch " Compton Dinah," who was also a winner on the bench.

The kennel of Mr. Herbert Mitchell, of Holly Bank, Bradford, has sent out a great number of Field Trial winners, both Pointers and Setters; lately, however, it has been represented by English Setters only. Some of the best from this kennel are " Lingfield Nell " (now in Russia), " Lingfield Kate," " Rapid Ranger of Bromfield," " Lingfield Beryl " (winner of the large sum of

" RAPID RANGER OF BROMFIELD."

£596 17s. 6d. in money at these Trials in just over two years), and " Lingfield Lally." These dogs are generally worked at the Trials by T. Lauder.

The South Wales kennel of Mr. A. T. Williams, whose dogs have the affix " of Gerwn," has in recent years had a really good record, not only in Setters, but also in Pointers and Retrievers.

Mr. A. N. Hall, of Chipping Norton, has some excellent working Setters, and they are put down at all the chief meetings. His " Gruinard Grampas " and " Gruinard Gloaming " being first and third in the All Aged Stakes at the Setter Club Meeting, near Thrapston, in 1909; he also won the Brace Stakes at the same meeting with "Gruinard Grebe" and "Gruinard Belle," besides many other stakes at the various trials.

The Hon. G. Lascelles has also run some good Setters; two particularly well remembered some few years ago were "Dora" and "Dart of Lyndhurst," handled by Frost, two very smart, active Setters.

The Setters of Mr. K. McDonall, of Stranraer, N.B., have always run very consistently at the chief meetings, and with success at a good many of them.

Mr. Isaac Sharpe, of Keith, Banffshire, N.B., has often brought some good working dogs at the Trials; these have, however, been generally Gordon Setters or Pointers. His Gordon, "Stylish Ranger" and the Pointer, "Stylish Shot," ran very well.

Mr. J. Frost ran two good Setters in 1909, "Lyddington Warren Rakeaway" and "Lyddington Warren Mystic," and they accounted for some good stakes.

In this short survey of the Field Trial Setters the writer has no doubt overlooked many good dogs, but most of those he has referred to have been seen by him at work.

R. R. P. WEARING.

191

WILLOW BROOK JOHN G., ENGLISH SETTER. Owned by Mr. Charles H. Tyler, of Ames Building, Boston. A great winner in America and as good a shooting dog as any. The Setter on winding game squats down and remains quite still.

Coloured illustrations in 1800 show very typical examples. The type of English Setter has altered very little if at all. They were used in early times to indicate the position of the game, to allow the man to arrange his net accordingly. (*See* Dr. Caius, p. 83).

THE ENGLISH SETTER*

The English Setter is very similar in type to the other varieties. Is white, marked with blue or black and liver, the marking being lightly put on. The coat is long, silky, and wavy ; the back of the legs is covered with long hair, standing out at right angles to the legs.

Instead of pointing, the setter ' sets,' i.e. squats down when noticing game. When worked in teams, the leading dogs sets to game, the team sets to him. They drop as if shot. The dogs remain absolutely still with their heads towards the game.

The head is clear-cut, with a long oval forehead, and long muzzle. The ears are covered with fine, silk-like hair, set low and hung in folds. The tip of the ear is velvety. The tail is carried in a straight line with the back. The English setter, apart from colour, varies from the Irish setter in having a longer head and squarer lips.

Before 1609, Setters were used to indicate the position of the game. The fowler then went forward and set his net. Even at that date the dogs were steady and reliable. Weight of dog 45 to 60 lb.

THE ENGLISH SETTER.

Head : Long and lean, with a **well-defined stop.** The **skull** oval from ear to ear, showing plenty of brain room, and with a well-defined occipital protuberance. The **muzzle** moderately deep and fairly square ; from the stop to the point of the nose should be long, the nostrils wide, and the jaws of nearly equal length, **flews not** to be pendulous ; **the colour** of the **nose** black, or dark, or light liver, according to the colour of the coat. The **eyes** bright, mild and intelligent, and of a dark-hazel colour—darker the better. The **ears** of moderate length, set on low and hanging in neat folds close to the cheek ; the tip velvety, the upper part clothed with fine silky hair. **Neck :** Rather long, muscular, and lean, slightly arched at the crest, and clean cut where it joins the head ; towards the shoulder larger, and very muscular, **not** throaty or any pendulosity below the throat, but elegant and blood-like in appearance. **Body :** Of moderate length, with shoulders well set back, or oblique ; **back** short and level ; **loins** wide, slightly arched, strong, and muscular. **Chest** deep in the brisket, with good round widely-sprung ribs, deep in the back ribs, that is, well ribbed up. **Legs and feet :** Stifles well bent and ragged, **thighs** long from hip to hock. The forearm big and very muscular, **the** elbow well let down. Pasterns short, muscular, and straight. The **feet** very close and compact, and well protected by hair between the toes.

The **tail** set on almost in a line with the back; medium length, not curly or ropy, to be slightly curved or scimitar-shaped, but with no tendency to turn upwards, the flag or feather hanging in long pendant flakes. The feather not commencing at the root, but slightly below, and increasing in length to the middle, then gradually tapering off towards the end ; and the hair long, bright, soft, and silky, wavy but not curly. **Coat and feathering :** The **coat** from the back of the head in a line with the ears to be slightly wavy, long and silky, which should be the case with the coat generally ; the breeches and forelegs, nearly down to the feet, well feathered. The **colour** either black and white, lemon and white, liver and white, or tri-colour—that is, black, white, and tan ; those without heavy patches of colour on the body but flecked all over preferred.

THE ENGLISH SETTER

Origin and History.—The English setter in the form now familiar to us received a marked impetus when in 1825 Edward Laverack purchased *Old Moll* and *Ponto* from the Rev. A. Harrison, who lived near Carlisle. Before we come to that period, however, it may be noted that Gervase Markham in "The Art of Fowling" (1655) described a dog that had at least the markings of the modern :

> "To speak then in a word touching the best choice of this Setting-dogge let him be as neere as you can the best bredde land-spaniell that you can procure : and though some have been curious in observing of their colours, as giving preheminence to the Motley, the lieur-hude or the white and black spotted."

Laverack, born at Keswick in 1800 and dying at Ash, near Whitchurch in Shropshire, 1877, was apprenticed to a shoemaker, but afterwards inherited money, and became the lessee of extensive moors. Of course, he was not the originator of the modern dog, for Mr. Harrison is said to have kept his pure for thirty-five years previously to the purchase mentioned, and other strains had also acquired fame. In the course of years,

197

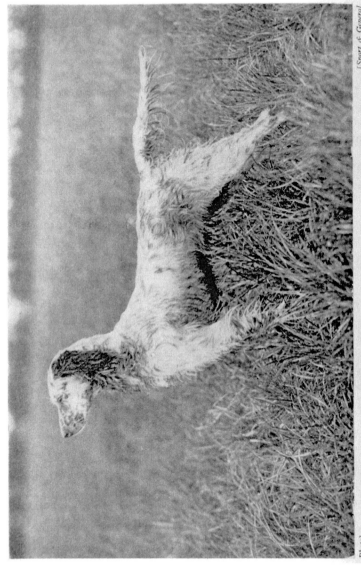

ENGLISH SETTER: *Jubee Vine of Bobbing*, the property of the late Mr. F. C. Lowe.

however, the Laverack setters established a reputation that had no rivals, and on his death, a stone was erected in the churchyard at Ash Parva, bearing this inscription : " To the memory of Edward Laverack ; born Keswick, 1800 ; died at Broughall Cottage, 1877. This monument is erected by admirers in England and America." On the reverse are the words : " His great love for the lower animals made him many friends. He was especially fond of dogs, and by careful selection remodelled the English setter, the best of which are known by his name."

The claims he made about his dogs being descended from the original pair in unsullied purity have since been regarded as extravagant. The occasional appearance of reds and blacks strengthened the belief that he had used an Irish setter cross, but for all that there cannot be much doubt that he inbred too closely, if cleverly, producing dogs of great beauty and wonderful field sense ; dogs that hunted with a high head, ranged well at a rare pace, had fine noses and so on.

This being so, what could have been the matter with them ? Well, they were incurably headstrong and difficult to break, and they passed on these faults to other strains. " Stonehenge," who was a contemporary, wrote :

> " Unfortunately this close breeding produced a great many idiots and delicate constitutions, but if only a Laverack puppy had his senses, his limbs of good formation, and escaped the ills of teething, distemper, etc., he was sure to be a good dog in the field *when well broken*, but he required a deal of this."

Overlapping with Mr. Laverack for a few years was that fine old Shropshire sportsman, the late Mr. R. Ll. Purcell Llewellin, who may be regarded as the greater force of the two, I think. He, too, loved a handsome dog that was a worker as well. In his early attempts at crossing English setters with Irish he produced some uncommonly handsome bench winners, the utilitarian qualities of which did not please him, and in 1871, by the purchase of Mr. Statters' *Dan*, and breeding him to Laverack bitches, he laid the foundations of his incomparable strain. The finest tribute one can pay him is that he placed his imprimatur so successfully on his dogs as to make them recognisable either at field trials, by their manner of working, or in the show ring by their appearance.

Mr. Llewellin disclosed the ingredients of his prescription in a letter dated 1912, after his young dog *Count Beau* had distinguished himself at field trials :

> " I am naturally proud to think that after nearly forty-five years of breeding this breed pure, without an out-cross, and winning more than my share with it during that time, I can still, at the eleventh hour, put into the field specimens of the same breed good enough to beat representatives of all that can be brought against them. That is the point I think most of. A blend formed by me many years ago of selected examples of South Esk, Laverack, and old Gordon blood (not the black-and-tan, so-called Gordons, but the black-white-and-tans of Beaufort Castle and Cawdor Castle). I have carefully kept these, thus crossed, up to the present day."

Further self-revelation was made in another letter to an American correspondent in 1916, in which Mr. Llewellin deplored the inferior type of most field-trial dogs and the poor working capacity of the show dogs. He proceeded :

> " I have always been handicapped all my life by trying, as far as I can, to combine type and working points. It is no easy matter, for I need not say a specialist has an easier task than one who attempts two opposite things ; and if I had simply ignored type, and gone, as my opponents do, for work alone, or ignored all working instincts and brains, and gone for show points alone, the task would have been far easier ; but I hate an ugly dog, and as I keep dogs more for pleasure, not coin, I can please myself ! I am an old man now, seventy-four,

and all who began with me are dead, or have given up dogs (for 'driving' is the fashionable shooting, and no dogs but Retrievers), but I am still old-fashioned enough to stick to the dogs without the shooting, rather than the shooting without the dogs. I have seen so many new men come in and blaze away for a few years, and then give it up."

Standard Description.—In appearance and disposition the English setter is very much to my liking. **Head.**—His long lean head, with a well-defined stop and fairly square muzzle, betokens intelligence and kindliness to a high degree, which is confirmed by the dark hazel-coloured eyes. The skull is oval from ear to ear, with well-defined occiput. **Body.**—The neck is rather long, muscular and lean, slightly arched at the crest and clean-cut where it joins the head. Towards the shoulder it should be larger and very muscular, but there should be no dewlap or pendulosity under the throat. The body is of moderate length, with shoulders well set back, the back short and level, and the wide, strong loins are slightly arched. The chest is deep in the brisket, with good, round, widely-sprung ribs, which are carried well back. The stifles are well bent and ragged, the thighs long from hip to hock. **Legs and Feet.**—The front legs should be muscular and straight, the feet close, compact and well protected by hair between the toes. **Tail.**—The tail is set on almost in a line with the back, is of medium length and must not be curly or ropey. Though it is slightly curved, scimitar fashion, there should be no tendency to turn upwards, the flag or feathering hanging in long pendant flakes. The feathering does not begin quite at the root, but slightly below, and increases in length to the middle, afterwards gradually tapering off towards the end. **Coat.**—The coat from the back of the head, in a line with the ears, ought to be slightly wavy, long and silky, which should be the case with the coat generally. Breeches and forelegs nearly down to the feet are well feathered. *Colour.*—Colours may be black-and-white, lemon-and-white, liver-and-white, or tricolour—that is, black-white-and-tan ; those that are without heavy patches of colour on the body but are flecked all over are preferred. These particulars are from the standard approved by the English Setter Club.

THE ENGLISH SETTER

203

THE ENGLISH SETTER

WE have various types of Setters, each of which possesses wonderful qualities, and although it is possible that originally they sprang from the same stock, it is difficult to definitely state which of them is the most useful as an all-round dog.

The English Setter, however, is a beautiful animal, and has much to commend it to sportsmen. Its proper sphere is amongst the root crops, when September arrives and the partridge season commences, or on the moors when the red grouse are in quest.

English Setters should have long lean heads, with a well-defined stop; skull oval from ear to ear, with plenty of brain room, and a well-defined occipital protuberance; muzzle fairly square and moderately

ENGLISH SETTER

deep; nostrils wide; flews not too pendulous; eyes dark hazel, the darker the better; body moderately long, with shoulders well set back or oblique; back short and level; loins wide, slightly arched, strong and muscular; deep brisket, with well-sprung ribs. Tail should be set on almost level with the back, medium length, not ropy or curly, with no tendency to turn upwards, the flag or feather hanging in long pendant flakes, feather to commence not at, but slightly below, the root, gradually increasing in length, and afterwards tapering off towards the end. Coat and feathering: the coat from the back of the head in a line with the ears ought to be slightly wavy, long and silky, well feathered on fore-legs; colour may be either black-and-white, liver-and-white, lemon-and-white, or tricolour, without heavy patches of colour on the body, but preferably flecked all over.

ENGLISH SETTERS

Mr. and Mrs. Eddington, of Dunelmy, one-time of the finest kennels of English Setters in the world.   Here is Mrs. Eddington, with some of her dogs.

205

A NOTED LAVERACK.

The famous Setter "Monk of Furness", one of Mr. Edward Laverack's noted dogs.

CH. "QUEEN ELSIE".

At the end of the nineteenth century this Spaniel bitch was one of the best Setters.
She was owned by Mr. M. G. Potter, of Carlisle.

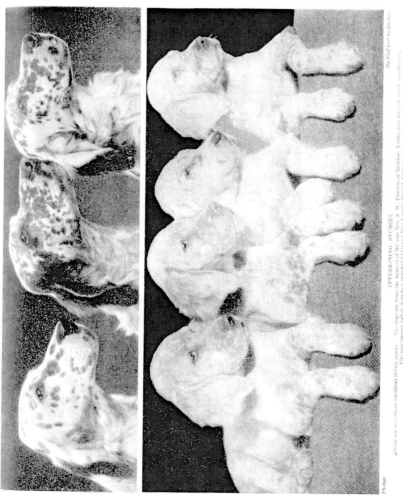

[Photo]

INTERESTING SETTER

A boot dog now three months' Setter bench. The dogs are from the kennels of Mr. and Mrs. A. W. Fluckes, of Ballidon, Yorks., and are just seven months old. The photograph below depicts a delightful litter of Blue Lewis's English Setter puppies.

[By Fall and by Guess.]

207

"BAILDON BARRA".
A remarkable Setter, showing the feather, or flag. It has won five first prizes, and is the property of Mrs. A. W. Rhodes.

"WITHINLEE GROWSE".
This fine English Setter was best in show on thirty-six occasions. It belongs to Mr. and Mrs. Edlington

208

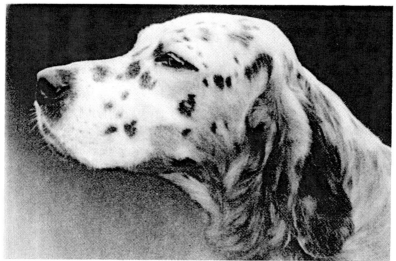

AN EXCELLENT HEAD.
This picture presents "Stainton Sultan", the property of Mr. T. H. Moorby, who owns a powerful kennel of Setters and Pointers.

Photo]   [Fall.

AT TWO MONTHS.

Setter puppies, as Spaniel puppies, are most fascinating. It must be hard for breeders having to part with them. Here are "Withinlee Wondergirl" and "Wonderlass", the property of Mr. and Mrs. Eadington.

210

THE BIRDS RISE

Joel McCrea is a famous American radio star, but ranching is his hobby and the gun his favourite sport. An English Setter works for him on his shooting expeditions

211

[Photo]

IN THE U.S.A. A kennel at Georgia is here seen exercising. Some of the dogs are very heavily marked, according to English standards.

The English setter is an important gun-dog in America.

[E.N.A.

TOGETHER.
Four charming English setters owned by the late Mr. R. E. Potter. The three on the right are particularly good specimens of the breed.

English Setter.

English Setter.—The English Setter is undoubtedly one of the most beautiful and elegant of the canine race, the varied colours are most attractive, and they are fast becoming a fashionable and favourite breed. This is largely due to the activities of the English and Gordon Setter Association, the Setter and Pointer Club, and the English Setter Club.

There are varied opinions as to the exact origin of the English Setter, but none of these are convincing or conclusive. It is believed that many centuries ago it was referred to as a Spaniel. In the year 1555, Robert, Duke of Northumberland, is said to have trained a Setter to set partridges in conjunction with the net, and it is quite possible that the dog of that period is the foundation of the English Setter of the present day. It appears that the first

IN ITALY.
Signor Mussolini owns this attractive team of English Setters and exhibited them recently at a show held by the Kennel Club of Rome.

authentic record of the English Setter, as we know it to-day, occurred in the time of the late Mr. Edward Laverack, who died in 1877, reputed to be the greatest authority on Setters of all times. He bred some magnificent dogs, and doubtless all our present-day Setters trace their origin to this strain.

The late Mr. Purcell Llewellin also did much for the breed, and was probably one of the greatest breeders we have had. He was most successful on the bench and was practically invincible in the field. It makes interesting reading to follow the number of wins at field trials of the Llewellin Setters in the early numbers of the Kennel Club stud books.

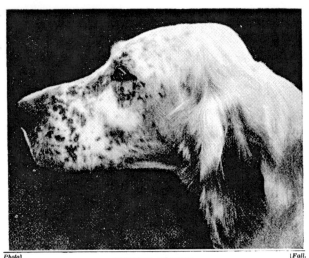

Photo]   "MAESYDD MAYFLY".   *[Fall.*

Mr. Edward Laverack agreed that the Setter was but an improved Spaniel. Mr. P. Llewellin bought his noted "Countess". He further improved the breed.

In the middle 'eighties Mr. George Potter, late Secretary of the English Setter Club, had many beautiful dogs, and his prefix "Wetherill" is found in many of the pedigrees to-day. Mr. F. C. Lowe's was also a name to be conjured with in the Setter world, and his dogs were most successful on the bench and in the field. Mention should be made of Mr. Elias Bishop, who was always well to the fore with his dogs, and of his nephew, Mr. Arch. Bishop, secretary of the English Setter Club.

One likes to think backwards over the—as one might call them—pillars of the breed. Of course, in the very early stages of the pure-bred "Blue Beltons" come Mr. Laverack's "Dash", Mr. Garth's "Daisy", Mr. Purcell Llewellin's "Countess", and Mr. Dickson's "Bella". The pedigree of Mr. Laverack's "Dash" makes history in a way. His sixty G-g-g-grandparents consist of four dogs only, which he used solely to perpetuate his strain. They were "Ponto", "Old Moll", "Dash 1st". and

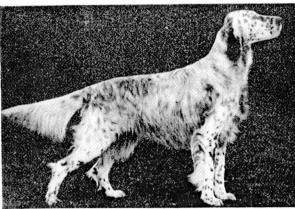

Photo]   "BAILDON BRACKEN".   *[Fall.*

Mr. A. W. Rhodes' dog shows the typical flecking of the Setter breed (note the front legs) which adds so much to their beauty. Notice, also, how the tail is set on, almost in line with the back.

214

TWO PETS.

English setters are not only good gun dogs, but make also excellent companions. Of gentle disposition, they are ideal as pets for children. Jackie Cooper, the world-famous boy film star, is here seen with his canine pal.

[Photo] IN SERIOUS MOOD. [Waller Guice

This English setter, "Punch of Fermanar", the property of Miss K. Lewis, is the proud winner of two Champion Certificates and four reserves.
Note how long and lean the head is, and how well defined the stop.

"Bella 1st". Later on one comes to the famous Llewellin dogs, the Wind'em's, of which a few survive to this day; in fact, the writer has a great-grand-daughter of "Nick Wind'em". Then comes the world-famous Mallwydd Kennel, owned by Mr. Tom Steadman. Although now retired from the show ring as an exhibitor, Mr. Steadman officiates as a judge at some of the championship shows. That grand bitch, Ch. "Mallwydd Sarah", and that great sire, Ch. "Mallwydd Albert", to mention only two, have left their mark in English Setter pedigrees. Mr. David Steadman is following his father's footsteps, and his prefix "Maesydd" is almost a household word in gun-dog circles.

Among the Setters of recent years that have set their stamp on the breed must be mentioned the late Professor T. Price's "O by Jingo", "Nan of Crombie", "Glaisnook Kate", and "Alice of Crombie"; Mr. C. Atkinson's Ch. "Crossfell"; Mr. D. Steadman's "Maesydd Minnie" and "Maesydd Mariner"; Mr. and Mrs. Smerdon's "Petersham Blue Knight"; and the writer's Ch. "Maesydd Mustard", "Withinlee Albert", and "Withinlee Fay", all of whose names figure largely in the pedigrees of the present-day English Setter.

Photo] [Fall.

AT FIVE MONTHS.
A hamper-load of lively English Setter puppies sired by "Withinlee Albert".

In the field trial world Mr. Isaac Sharpe's Stylish Kennel, Capt. Blaine's West Down Kennels, and Mr. Mitchell's Lingfield Kennels are generally predominant.

The popularity of the English Setter has, within recent years, grown very rapidly, and the registrations are steadily increasing. The reason for this is plain to see. The animal's beauty is beyond question; its grace and elegance give it distinction; it is an ideal companion, and possesses a most amiable disposition. It has been proved over and over again that as a gun-dog it is equal to any. As a show dog it is always popular, attracts attention, and is seldom shy. Nowadays there are few show secretaries who do not cater for this breed: a good English Setter is outstanding, and it is not uncommon to see it winning "best in show". The English Setter is less excitable than its Irish cousin; is most intelligent, and easy to train, and is a real, true, affectionate pal, devoid of vice and never ferocious. Those who have once owned one, either as a companion, show dog, or for the gun, seldom take kindly to any other breed.

One often hears from the field trial habitués that the present show type is of little or no use as a worker. It is a pity that more English Setters

Photo] [Fall.

IN THE YOUNGER SET.
Four youngsters from Mr. and Mrs. W. R. Eadington's kennels. Note the nice flecking of the three on the right. It is surprising that the English Setter is not more often kept as a pet, for a better-tempered dog it would be difficult to find.

217

are not more consistently worked, not necessarily at field trials, but for ordinary shooting. Given the opportunity, the show Setter would hold its own with any. The future of the breed demands attention to the working side if one looks at it from a commercial standpoint alone : at the present time the demand far exceeds the supply.

Undoubtedly one of the principal requirements in Setters is style of movement, which should be quick, easy and true ; a dog with a rheumatic style of movement is most objectionable and is little use as a field trial or show dog. There is a tendency however, to-day, to exaggerate the head qualities at the expense of the rest of the body. This is to be greatly deplored, in spite of the fact that a well-known judge once made the remark that the head was the first and last thing seen when examining a dog. A Setter, to be an object of beauty, must be symmetrical and should have no exaggerated points ; let the dog as a whole be so constructed on sound lines that there is no jarring element to the eye, and one that is capable of doing a good day's work.

The demand from abroad for this now popular breed is rapidly increasing. It is a variety with prospects of a bright and popular future. The writer's conception of a perfect English Setter is as follow : A dog of medium size, neither too large nor too small ; lightly ticked by blue, blue-and-tan, or lemon ; free from heavy dark patches or solid

Photo]   *[Fall.*
"CARSWELL MIMORU".
This head study of Miss P. M. Butler's dog well illustrates the occipital protuberance that is so marked in the Setter

colouring. A head that is long, without exaggeration, beautifully chiselled, and with that wonderful expression only to be found in an English Setter, namely, a combination of sadness, intelligence, and dignity ; and a clean, long, muscular neck set on to fine sloping shoulders. The shoulders should be just slightly higher in outline than the hindquarters ; the front sound and not too narrow ; the brisket deep ; and the ribs well sprung ; a shortish back ; well-developed hindquarters ; thighs long, short hocks ; the tail well set on, and not too long. Add to this, silky feathering on tail, chest and forelegs, and the result is one of the most beautiful dogs in existence. To appreciate the beauty of an English Setter one should see it ranging a moor in September, when the heather is out, and the sight of a light blue belton-and-tan setting at grouse is a delight.

By courtesy]   *[W. R. Eadington*
CH. "MAESYDD MUSTARD".
This very beautiful dog won his championship. Champions are rare in the world of sporting dogs, for they must excel in the field : they must be workers as well as good to look at.

218

"WITHINLEE TANGO".
This fine Setter, the winner of numerous prizes, is owned by Mr. and Mrs. W. H. Eadington.

CH. "PENNINE PATRON".
A well-built Setter, the property of Mr. H. E. Whitwell, showing most excellent body shape.

GENERAL IMPRESSION.—Unintelligent appearance The Bloodhound type, with heavy and big head and ears and clumsy body ; as well as the Collie type, with its pointed muzzle and curved tail.

HEAD.—Pointed, snipy, dropping or upturned muzzle, coarse heads, and short foreface.

EYES.—Too light in colour, too deep-set, or too prominent.

EARS.—Set too high, or unusually broad or heavy.

NECK.—Thick and short ; throatiness.

defined stop. The skull oval from ear to ear, showing plenty of brain room, and with a well-defined occipital protuberance. The muzzle moderately deep and fairly square ; from the stop to the point of the nose should be long, the nostrils wide, and the jaws of nearly equal length, flews not to be pendulous ; the colour of the nose should be black, or dark, or light liver, according to the colour of the coat. The eyes should be bright, mild and intelligent, and of a dark hazel colour, harmonizing with the colour of the coat. The ears of moderate length, set on low, and hanging in neat folds close to the

Photo]   "WITHINLEE WONDER".   *[Fall*

Another Setter, the property of Mr. and Mrs. Fadington, a dog with plenty of heart room and good head. The breed at one time was taught to go down, but to-day they point in the same manner as the Pointer.

SHOULDERS AND BACK.—Irregularly formed, back too long.

CHEST.—Too broad.

LEGS AND FEET.- Crooked legs ; out-turned elbows ; the toes scattered ; flat-footed ; short, stumpy legs ; stiff or stilted hind action.

TAIL.—Too long, badly carried, or hooked at the end.

COAT.—Very broken or curly, with dry, lustreless appearance.

COLOUR.—Heavy patches of colour on the body very undesirable.

DESCRIPTION AS ADOPTED BY THE ENGLISH AND GORDON SETTER ASSOCIATION.

HEAD.—Should be long and lean, with a well-

cheek ; the tip should be velvety, the upper part clothed with fine silky hair. As a guide, the length of head for dogs about 10 inches. and about 9 inches for bitches.

NECK.—Should be rather long, muscular, and lean, slightly arched at the crest, and clean-cut where it joins the head ; towards the shoulder it should be larger, and very muscular, not throaty ; nor should there be any pendulosity below the throat, but elegant and blood-like appearance.

BODY.— Should be of moderate length, with shoulders well set back or oblique ; shoulders should be slightly higher than the loin ; loins wide, slightly arched, strong, and muscular. Chest deep in the brisket with good. round, widely

220

"REX OF CROMDIE".

The leather of a Setter is an outstanding feature of the breed, and Mr. A. B. Nicholson's dog, "Rex", presents a good example. The English Setter was already popular at the commencement of the nineteenth century.

"BAYLDOME THATCHER".

Truly a Setter is a magnificent dog. The one shown immediately above belongs to Mr. A. W. Rhodes and is lightly flecked all over.

sprung ribs, deep in the back ribs—that is, well ribbed up.

LEGS AND FEET.—Stifles well bent and ragged ; thighs long from hip to hock. The forearm big and very muscular, the elbow well let down. Pasterns short, muscular, and straight. The feet very close and compact, and well protected with hair between the toes.

TAIL.—The tail should be set on almost in line with the back ; medium length, not curly or ropy ; to be slightly curved or scimitar-shaped, but with no tendency to turn upwards ; the flag or feather hanging in long pendant flakes. The feather should not commence at the root, but slightly below, and increase in length to the middle, then gradually taper off towards the end ; and the hair long, bright, soft and silky, wavy but not curly.

COAT AND FEATHERING. — The coat from the back of the head in a line with the ears ought to be slightly wavy, long and silky, which should be the case

Photo] AT ATTENTION. *[Fall*

Mr. H. E. Whitwell's "Fantail" in an attitude that seems to indicate it is waiting for the next order. Note the tense and expectant expression in the eyes.

with the coat generally ; the breeches and forelegs, nearly down to the feet, should be well feathered.

COLOUR AND MARKINGS.—The colour may be either blue-and-white, lemon-and-white, liver-and-white, or tricolour—that is, blue, white, and tan ; the lighter the better ; heavy patches of colour very undesirable.

SIZE.—As a guide to size : shoulder height for dogs, 24 to 25½ inches ; for bitches, 22 to 24 inches.

222

[Keeyes]

ENGLISH SETTER.

[Fall.

Miss K. Lewis's Ch. "Stylehurst Punch of Fermanar" was bred by Miss E. A. Rumball from Ch. "Maesydd Mustard" and "Stylehurst Cowslip". Born in June 1931, it is one of the oustanding members of the famous Fermanar Kennels.

THE ENGLISH SETTER
STYLEHURST PUNCH
OF FERMANAR

The English Setter is one of the most beautiful dogs shown at the present time; the varied colouring, apart from their dignity, makes them very attractive, so much so that they are not only a fashionable breed but are great favourites among the sporting fraternity.

Although the breed has been known in this country for some hundreds of years, the type known to-day are a distinct improvement on their forbears, but the original function of the " Setter," after suitable training, are brought into prominence and they become ideal gun dogs.

The English Setter is considered to be less temperamental than his Irish cousin, possesses no vices, and is true and affectionate, and from the experience of the author seldom, if ever, takes to another owner.

There are four types of colour and markings. Blue and white, lemon and white, liver and white, and tricolour; that is, tan, white and blue, the lighter the better. Heavy splashes of one colour are not so attractive.

Before an English Setter can aspire to Championship status he must pass successfully through Field Trials.

THE ENGLISH SETTER   Gay Lad of Gwynfryn

THE ENGLISH SETTER   Puppies, Fermanar Strain

THE ENGLISH SETTER

STYLEHURST PUNCH AND JUDY
(OLD FERMANAR)

THE ENGLISH SETTER   " Fermanar " Puppies

THE ENGLISH SETTER   A Quartette of " Fermanars "

CPSIA information can be obtained at www.ICGtesting.com
Printed in the USA
LVOW12s0931021014

406847LV00001B/28/P

9 781445 525983